# HISTORY & GEOGRAPHY 809
## Cold War America (1945–1990)

**LIFEPAC Test is located in the center of the booklet.** Please remove before starting the unit.

**Author:**
Theresa Buskey, B.A., J.D.

**Editor:**
Alan Christopherson, M.S.

**Westover Studios Design Team:**
Phillip Pettet, Creative Lead
Teresa Davis, DTP Lead
Nick Castro
Andi Graham
Jerry Wingo

**Alpha Omega**
PUBLICATIONS

**804 N. 2nd Ave. E.**
**Rock Rapids, IA 51246-1759**

# Cold War America (1945–1990)

## Introduction

From 1945 to 1991, the U.S. and the Union of Soviet Socialist Republics (U.S.S.R.) met in a conflict called the "Cold War." It was a conflict of ideas, economics, propaganda, and intimidation. During all of those years, the two sides never directly fought each other in a "hot" war. However, during those years, international politics revolved around the confrontation between the two super powers.

One of the most important features of the Cold War was a massive arms race, particularly in the area of atomic weapons. By the end of the era, both sides had enough nuclear bombs to destroy all life on earth. This "mutually assured destruction," the ability of both sides to destroy the other if the bombs were ever used, was one of the main reasons the two sides never quite went to war. Both sides were aware that a U.S.-Soviet war could be the end for everyone on the planet.

The Cold War was a world war. Each super-power could count on the support of allies or satellites all over the world. Both fought tenaciously for the hearts of the non-aligned (neutral) nations. Civil wars became part of the Cold War as the Soviets and the Americans supported different sides. However, even in "hot" wars like Korea and Vietnam, the two great powers were careful to avoid expanding the wars beyond that place. These were "limited" wars, carefully restricted to prevent the dreaded World War III.

At the heart of the conflict was the difference between the ideas of the two sides. America was a republic that favored freedom of ideas and a free market economic system. The Soviet Union was a communist nation. Communism is a system that allows no freedom of thought and has an economy completely owned and run by the government. Moreover, communism is a system of flagrant lies. Its governments claim they are utopias where the workers have everything they need, when in reality, people barely have enough of anything. The truth about corruption, poverty, inefficiency, and failure is never reported. Eventually, communism collapsed in the Soviet Union under the weight of its own stupidity. That collapse finally ended the Cold War

## Objectives

Read these objectives. The objectives tell you what you will be able to do when you have successfully completed this LIFEPAC. When you have finished this LIFEPAC, you should be able to:

1.  Describe the course of the Cold War and the incidents within it.

2.  Name the presidents of the Cold War and the events that happened during their administration.

3.  Describe the course of the Civil Rights Movement.

4.  Describe events in America and changes in American thinking during the Cold War era.

5.  Name the important people on both sides of the Cold War.

Survey the LIFEPAC. Ask yourself some questions about this study and write your questions here.

_____

_____

_____

_____

_____

_____

_____

_____

_____

_____

_____

_____

_____

_____

_____

_____

_____

_____

_____

_____

_____

# 1. HOT OR COLD?

The Cold War developed very quickly after World War II. Americans thought the Soviets would be willing to work with their allies after the defeat of Germany. Events quickly proved that assumption wrong.

Stalin was obsessed with protecting his nation by creating a buffer of loyal nations in Eastern Europe. Because these countries were occupied by Soviet troops, the Western nations could not stop it, except by starting another war. Stalin ignored his wartime promises and set up communist governments all over East Europe without allowing free elections.

These actions of Soviet aggression in the Middle East convinced America to abandon her traditional isolation. There was a very real fear that without the support of the United States, much of the world might be forced under the control of a communist dictatorship. Therefore, America took the leadership of the free world to contain communism at all costs.

The threat communism posed to the free world dominated American policy and thinking for forty-five years. It was especially strong in the first half of the era, up until the 1970s. During this time, the line between cold and hot war was often dangerously thin. Two "limited" wars were fought between communist and non-communist forces in Korea and Vietnam. Incidents like the Berlin blockade, the Berlin Wall, and the Cuban Missile Crisis threatened to escalate to war. The danger of an earth-destroying war was all too real.

## SECTION OBJECTIVES

**Review these objectives**. When you have completed this section, you should be able to:

1. Describe the course of the Cold War and the incidents within it.
2. Name the presidents of the Cold War and the events that happened during their administration.
4. Describe events in America and changes in American thinking during the Cold War era.
5. Name the important people on both sides of the Cold War.

## VOCABULARY

**Study these words to enhance your learning success in this section**.

**espionage** (es′ pē ə näzh). The use of spies to obtain information about the plans of a foreign government.

*fait accompli* (fāt′ ak om plē′). A thing accomplished and presumably irreversible.

**ideology** (īd ē äl′ ə jē). A systematic body of concepts about human life or culture.

**summit** (səm′ ət). A conference of the highest-level officials (such as heads of government).

**Note:** *All vocabulary words in this LIFEPAC appear in* **boldface** *print the first time they are used. If you are not sure of the meaning when you are reading, study the definitions given.*

**Pronunciation Key:** hat, āge, cãre, fär; let, ēqual, tėrm; it, īce; hot, ōpen, ôrder; oil; out; cup, pùt, rüle; child; long; thin; /ŦH/ for then; /zh/ for meaſure; /ə/ represents /a/ in about, /e/ in taken, /i/ in pencil, /o/ in lemon, and /u/ in circus.

# AMERICA from 1945 to 1990

**Harry S. Truman**
*1945-1953*
Democratic

**Dwight D. Eisenhower**
*1953-1961*
Republican

**John F. Kennedy***
*1961-1963*
Democratic

**Lyndon B. Johnson**
*1963-1969*
Democratic

**Richard M. Nixon**
*1969-1974*
Republican

**Gerald R. Ford**
*1974-1977*
Republican

**James E. Carter**
*1977-1981*
Democratic

**Ronald Reagan**
*1981-1989*
Republican

**George H. W. Bush**
*1989-1993*
Republican

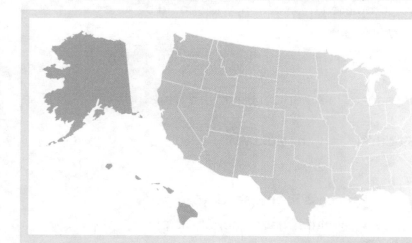

## STATES ADMITTED TO THE UNION

**Alaska**  1959
**Hawaii**  1959

## POPULATION of the United States of America

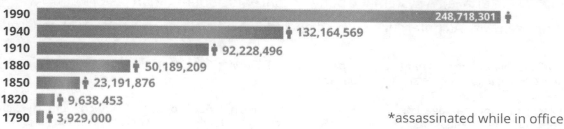

| Year | Population |
|---|---|
| 1990 | 248,718,301 |
| 1940 | 132,164,569 |
| 1910 | 92,228,496 |
| 1880 | 50,189,209 |
| 1850 | 23,191,876 |
| 1820 | 9,638,453 |
| 1790 | 3,929,000 |

*assassinated while in office

## Origins of the Cold War

**Harry S. Truman (1884-1972).** Harry S. Truman was unprepared when he suddenly became president in 1945 upon the death of Franklin Roosevelt. He knew nothing of foreign policy and had not been kept up-to-date on anything the president was doing. He did not even know about the project to develop the atomic bomb before Roosevelt's death. Yet, he managed to face his own ignorance and rose to be considered, by some, among America's best presidents.

Harry Truman was born and lived most of his life in Missouri. He was widely read but never obtained a college degree. After high school, he worked at various jobs until 1917. He was an artillery officer in France during World War I. After the war, he tried his hand at business and failed. He became a county official with the support of the powerful Democratic Party boss in Missouri, Tom Pendergast. In spite of his association with the corrupt Pendergast machine, Truman was honest and remained free from scandal.

With the help of the Pendergast machine, Truman was elected to the U.S. Senate in 1934 and 1940. He rose to national prominence as the head of a Senate committee that worked to uncover inefficiency and waste in government war spending. The Truman Commission (as it was called) saved the government about $15 billion. He was a compromise candidate for the vice presidency in 1944. In spite of his difficult start, Truman would set American policy that would affect the whole course of the Cold War.

**United Nations.** Roosevelt had been determined to replace the toothless League of Nations after World War II. Roosevelt had also learned from Wilson's mistakes. The American delegation to negotiate the charter included Senators from both parties and it was not tied to a harsh treaty. The conference to write a charter for the new United Nations opened in San Francisco on April 25, 1945, just two weeks after the death of F.D.R. The charter was written in nine weeks by representatives from about fifty nations. The U.S. Senate approved it in a matter of days.

The United Nations was set up with a general assembly in which all nations have a say and a smaller Security Council that controls major decisions on international disputes. The U.S., U.S.S.R., Britain, France, and China all were given permanent seats on the Security Council. The council must unanimously agree on any decision, which gives any one council member veto power over decisions. The Soviets made regular use of their veto in the early years of the U.N. to block any action they believed was threatening to their power (over 100 times in the first 25 years). This was one factor in the rapid growth of distrust between the allies after the end of World War II.

**Post-War Problems.** American hopes that the wartime cooperation with the Soviets would continue into the post-war era were quickly dashed. Relations with the Soviets went downhill after the understanding established at Yalta in early 1945. The Soviets quickly established obedient communist governments in Poland, Hungary, Bulgaria, and Romania. Communist governments came to power on their own in Yugoslavia and Albania. The democratic government that took control in Czechoslovakia was overthrown by the communists in 1948. The borders of the U.S.S.R. and its new "satellite" nations were closed to prevent the contamination of communist lies by contact with the truth from the outside world.

Germany and Berlin, its capital, had been divided into four sections occupied by the Soviets, Americans, British, and French. The four sectors were supposed to work together and eventually be reunited under an elected government. From the beginning, the Soviets refused to work with their allies to reunite the nation. They held the agricultural section in the East and refused to ship food to the other areas. They also stripped their section of all valuable industries, transporting whole factories to the U.S.S.R. They refused to sign a treaty with Germany, which would require them to withdraw, and the Soviets set up a communist government in their section.

In the end, the three Western powers worked to unite their sectors as best they could. As the Soviets became more threatening, the Western powers softened their attitude toward Germany, realizing they would need to rebuild the nation to aid in blocking communism. Eventually, two separate nations, communist East Germany and free West Germany would be created out of the defeated Nazi nation.

In 1946 the Soviets refused to remove their troops from Iran, instead using them to aid a separatist movement in the north. The Soviets hoped to gain control over some of the vast oil wealth of the nation. America took the issue to the U.N. and threatened to use force. Stalin backed down as he was not willing to start a war.

American statesmen realized it was only a matter of time until the Soviet Union had its own atomic bomb. These statesmen wanted to avoid a deadly arms race. So, in 1946, when the U.S. was the only nation with the bomb, they proposed giving this technology to the U.N. for international control. The proposal (the Baruch Plan) would have given the U.N. the power to inspect all nuclear sites in the world and insure that the technology was only being used for peaceful purposes. The Soviet Union refused to open its nuclear sites (present or future) to inspectors and used its veto to stop the plan.

**Containment**. In 1947 the Soviet Union was pressuring Turkey to give them bases and control of the Dardanelles, the straits leading to the Black Sea and the southern Soviet ports. The Soviets were also supporting a communist revolt in Greece. Britain had traditionally been the Western power that handled crises in the

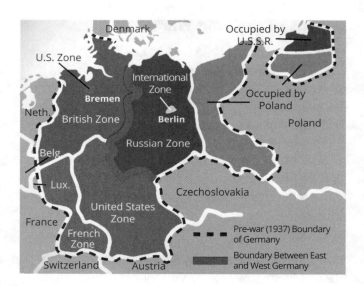

Mediterranean. Devastated by the war, Britain informed the U.S. that they no longer could bear the cost of defending those two nations against Soviet aggression.

Truman faced a key decision. Should the U.S. step in to stop communism in Greece and Turkey, or follow its tradition by not getting involved in Europe? He decided in favor of action. This decision set the course for the U.S. to actively oppose Soviet expansion for the duration of the Cold War.

Truman went before Congress in March of 1947 and asked for $400 million in aid for Greece and Turkey to prevent them from falling to a communist dictatorship. He knew that another war to end communism was out of the question. What he proposed was a policy recommended by an American diplomat, George Kernan. Kernan, who was an expert on the Soviet Union, recommended a steady, patient "containment" of Soviet expansion. If the communists were met with stable, forceful actions that prevented their expansion, they would be forced to calm down or rethink their policies, he believed.

Truman announced that it would be the policy of the U.S. to contain communism where it already existed. America would aid any free nation in the world faced with communist

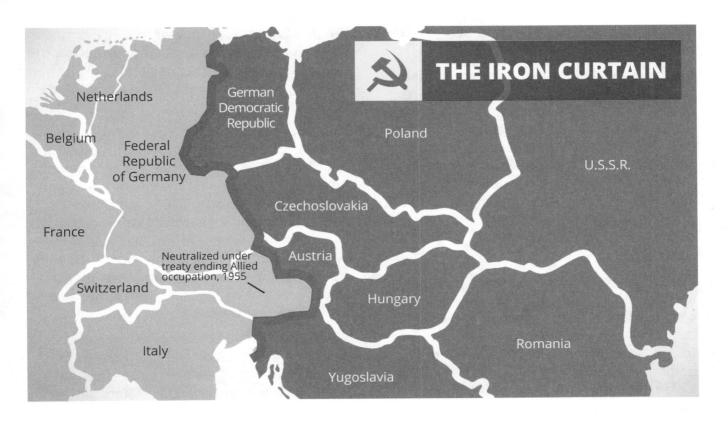

**THE IRON CURTAIN**

Netherlands

Belgium

France

Switzerland

Federal
Republic
of Germany

German
Democratic
Republic

Poland

U.S.S.R.

Czechoslovakia

Neutralized under
treaty ending Allied
occupation, 1955

Austria

Italy

Hungary

Yugoslavia

Romania

threats. This Containment Policy, or the Truman Doctrine, would be the foundation of all American policy toward communism during the Cold War. It would have both positive and negative results. American aid would keep many free people from facing the grinding oppression of a communist takeover. However, many petty dictators would receive U.S. aid to enhance their personal power simply because their opponents supported communist ideals or were receiving Soviet aid. It was a good policy in principle, but often unjust in how it was used.

**Marshall Plan**. Congress, with the support of the American people, approved the aid to Greece and Turkey. Both of these nations overcame their communist threats with the American help. Then, Truman turned his sights on the rest of Europe. The continent was not recovering from the devastation of the war. Communist parties, which were strong in times of economic problems because they promise to control the economy, were threatening to win elections in France and Italy.

George Marshall, who had run the war from Washington, was now Truman's secretary of state. He invited the nations of Europe to put together a plan for their recovery and the U.S. would supply the funds for it. Western Europe jumped at the offer. A conference in July of 1947 in Paris worked out the European end of the deal. The Soviet Union refused to allow its satellites to participate, calling the plan a capitalist plot. The U.S. Congress was reluctant to approve the Marshall Plan until February of 1948 when the head of the Czech democracy died mysteriously and the communists took over the nation. Congress authorized the funds.

The Marshall Plan was an incredible success. Within a few years, the Western nations were producing as much or more than they had before the war. The communists in France and Italy lost much of their popular support. Trade with Europe helped the American economy return to peacetime production. The Marshall Plan destroyed Soviet hopes of expanding into Western Europe. The strong, healthy Western democracies would not be susceptible to communist pressure, short of war.

**Berlin Airlift**. The Western powers continued to press forward with reforms in their sectors of Germany. In 1948 over strong Soviet objections, they set up currency reforms to aid the economy. The Soviets retaliated by cutting off all land routes to the American, French, and British sections of Berlin, inside the Soviet sector. The Soviets undoubtedly hoped to drive the democracies out of the city and bring it completely under Soviet control.

The U.S. refused to back down or start a war. Instead, American pilots began to fly supplies into the city. For almost a year, every piece of coal needed for heat, every cup of flour needed for bread, and every drop of medicine needed for the hospitals came in by plane. At the high point of the airlift, "Operation Vittles" landed a plane in Berlin once every three minutes around the clock. If a plane missed its landing on the first pass, it had to return to its home base. There were no openings on the runway for another try. The Soviets dropped the blockade in May of 1949.

**NATO**. The continuous aggressive action by the Soviets pushed the Western nations of Europe to sign a defensive treaty in 1948. Seeking security for itself and Europe, America was drawn into the alliance. In April of 1949, the United States broke 150 years of tradition when it signed a permanent alliance with eleven other Western democracies. The North Atlantic Treaty Organization (NATO) bound the nations to treat an attack on one nation as an attack on all. It was the first permanent alliance signed by the U.S. since the alliance with France during the Revolution. NATO was an apt symbol of the dramatic change in American thinking. She had now fully replaced Britain as the leader of the Western world.

**Iron Curtain**. By 1948, it was clear that the world had been divided into two armed camps. America led the free, wealthy Western democracies. They were called the Western Bloc and the Free or First World. The Soviet Union led the Communist nations which were referred to as the Communist or Eastern Bloc and as the Second World. Eventually, the poorer, developing nations of Africa, Asia, and Latin America, which were not clearly allied with either side, would be known as the Third World.

Winston Churchill, Britain's wartime leader, described the situation with his usual eloquence in March of 1946. In a speech at an American university Churchill stated: "an iron curtain has descended across the Continent" of Europe. The term "behind the Iron Curtain" was used throughout the Cold War to refer to the communist nations of Europe.

The United States made one basic assumption about communism during these early years. American leaders assumed that all communist nations and movements were under Soviet control. Many were, but not all. The U.S. was slow to realize that some revolutions that had Soviet support were not under perfect Soviet control. The U.S. also was slow to recognize differences between communist leaders of different nations. This "us against them" mentality limited American diplomatic choices for many years.

**Name the person, treaty, or item.**

1.1 _____    the two systems of government in conflict during
the Cold War

_____

1.2 _____    group that makes the major international decisions
at the U.N.

1.3 _____    basic American policy toward communism

1.4 _____    American reaction to the blockade of Berlin, 1948-49

1.5 _____    America's first permanent alliance since the
Revolution

1.6 _____    President who set the basic American policies for
the Cold War

1.7 _____    aid plan that restored post-war Western Europe

1.8 _____    barrier between the Free and Communist Worlds in
Europe, named by Winston Churchill

1.9 _____    first two nations given U.S. aid to stop communism
after World War II

_____

1.10 _____    international organization created in 1945

1.11 _____    proposal in 1946 to put atomic power under U.N.
control

**Complete these items.**

1.12 How was Germany administered in the years right after the war? _____

_____

_____

_____

1.13 How did Germany wind up as two nations for the duration of the Cold War? _____

_____

_____

_____

1.14 What event in 1948 pushed Congress to approve the Marshall Plan? _____

_____

**1.15** Name the nations of Eastern Europe that became communist after the war. _____

_____

_____

**1.16** Name two Soviet actions in 1946 that pushed the world toward the Cold War. _____

_____

_____

**1.17** Identify each of these groups.

a. Western Bloc _____

b. Eastern Bloc _____

c. Third World _____

**1.18** Describe the Truman Doctrine. _____

_____

_____

**1.19** In your own words, describe why the Cold War developed after World War II? _____

_____

_____

_____

## Heating Up, Cooling Down

**1949**. 1949 was a bad year for the Western Bloc. The Soviet Union exploded its first atomic bomb that year. American experts had been expecting this, but not so soon. The Soviet nuclear program was aided by communist **espionage** in America. The two superpowers immediately began to pour money into bigger and more sophisticated nuclear weapons to make sure their opponents never had an advantage over them. Both sides also realized that a war between the two Blocs now had the potential for destruction beyond anything ever seen before. They would have to make certain that war never started.

Also in 1949, America's ally in China, Chiang Kai-shek, lost in a civil war to the communist forces under Mao Zedong. Chiang's government (Nationalist China) was hopelessly corrupt and never was able to win the support of the huge peasant population, which followed Mao. American policymakers decided there was no way to prevent the loss if Chiang could not get the support of his own people. Chiang and the Nationalists fled to the island of Taiwan to live under American protection. America refused to recognize the new communist government and insisted for years that the Nationalists on Taiwan were the rightful rulers of China.

Mao was a charismatic leader and a different kind of communist than Stalin. Mao saw communism as a continuous revolution to bring his kind of "equality" to all people by force. Stalin was more practical, more interested in simple power than ideas. The Soviets gave the Chinese communists economic and military aid for years, but the two sides eventually came to distrust each other. In time, communist Russia and communist China would actually fight along their border. However, it was years before the U.S. took advantage of this split.

In the meantime, rabid anti-communists in America demanded to know how we had "lost" China. Some charged that communist spies and sympathizers in the government had blocked the U.S. from giving the Nationalists the support they needed. The intense public reaction to the success of communism in China made future presidents very fearful of "losing" any more countries.

**Korean War**. The Soviet Union occupied the northern part of the Korean Peninsula after it declared war on Japan in the final days of World War II. The Americans occupied the southern part of the country, below the 38th parallel. Just as in Europe, Stalin set up a communist government in his section while the Americans established a democracy in theirs. The two sides each claimed to be the legitimate government of the whole nation and threatened to attack the other.

The U.S. eventually pulled its soldiers out of Korea and made statements that implied they would not protect the South. On June 25, 1950, the North attacked and quickly drove the smaller Southern army back. It appears, from the murky evidence, that Stalin did not plan the attack, but he did approve it. He probably thought his ally could win a quick, painless victory that the U.S. would be forced to accept as a *fait accompli*. He had not counted on Truman, the U.N., and MacArthur.

Truman was determined to defend his containment policy. If the communists were allowed to succeed with this kind of blatant armed attack in Korea, there was a serious concern they would try it in other places, like Europe. The president appealed to the United Nations. The Soviets were boycotting the Security Council because the Chinese seat was still held by the Nationalists of Taiwan. Without fear of a

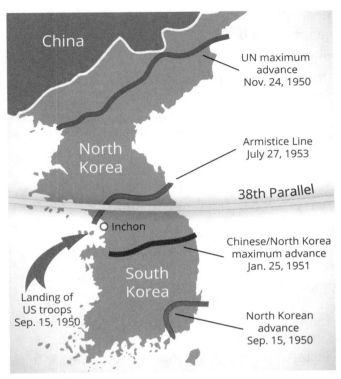

| The Korean War

Soviet veto, the U.N. condemned the invasion and requested its members send troops to aid South Korea. Truman immediately sent American forces at the command of General Douglas MacArthur. Eventually, sixteen nations would send troops to aid the South, but South Korea and the U.S. would do most of the fighting.

MacArthur and the South Koreans were pushed back until they set up an effective defensive line around the city of Pusan. The Pusan Perimeter barely held the southeast corner of the peninsula. Then, MacArthur launched a brilliant amphibious landing at Inchon, behind the enemy lines, in September of 1950. The Northern lines collapsed and they retreated to their own territory. MacArthur pursued them and pushed north almost to the Chinese border by November.

MacArthur arrogantly dismissed any threat from the communist Chinese as his army came closer to their border. However, the Chinese sent in thousands of "volunteers" who drove the Americans back behind the 38th parallel yet again. Counterattacks stabilized the battle lines near the old border. The two sides remained stalemated there for the rest of the war.

Stung by his defeat, MacArthur wanted to bomb and blockade China, but Truman and his military superiors believed that might start World War III. They were willing to settle for the recovery of South Korea, communism would be contained without a world war. So, once the U.N. forces were back to the 38th parallel, Truman offered to open negotiations.

MacArthur was contemptuous of Truman's approach to the war. The arrogant general wanted a total victory over communism. He made threats against China and sent letters to Congress openly disputing the decisions of his superiors. One of the greatest threats to any democracy is a military that will not obey the elected leaders. MacArthur went too far, and Truman had the courage to fire him for insubordination in April, 1951.

The United States was violently anti-communist in 1951 and MacArthur was incredibly popular. He came home to a hero's welcome in the States. Truman, on the other hand, was so unpopular he could have been impeached easily if some grounds had been found. However, MacArthur's popular support did not survive a Congressional investigation. It quickly became clear that the military leadership in Washington agreed with Truman. None of them wanted to risk a war with China that could easily draw in the Soviet Union, just to the north. General Omar Bradley testified that MacArthur's plan would "involve us in the wrong war, at the wrong place, at the wrong time, and with the wrong enemy."

Peace talks opened in July of 1951 at a village near the 38th parallel. They quickly stuck over the issue of returning prisoners– repatriation. Many of the prisoners did not want to go home and the U.N. was not willing to force them to do so. The communists insisted that the all prisoners must go home whether they wanted to or

| Nikita Khrushchev

not! They did not want the public embarrassment of having many of their soldiers refuse. It would show that their countries were not a paradise as communist propaganda claimed. Over this issue, the talks stalled for two years while men continued to die.

Finally, in March of 1953, Stalin died. The new leadership in the Kremlin, the Soviet capital building, softened its tone somewhat. The newly elected U.S. president, Dwight D. Eisenhower, pushed for peace. As a result, an armistice was finally signed in July of 1953. Repatriation was voluntary, but each nation was allowed to visit the men who refused. About 14,000 Chinese, 7,600 N. Koreans, 325 S. Koreans, 21 Americans, and 1 British refused repatriation. A de-militarized zone was set up along the 38th parallel, but a final peace treaty to end the war was never signed.

**Tensions**. Tension continued between the two super powers after Korea. America set off a hydrogen bomb (a more powerful atomic weapon) in 1952. The Soviets followed quickly. In 1953 Soviet troops suppressed a rebellion in East Germany. In 1955 the Eastern Bloc created its own "defensive" alliance called the Warsaw Pact to counter NATO. Since communist **ideology** was to take over the world, these incidents kept the U.S. very nervous about Soviet actions and intentions.

For America, the bitterest failure of the Cold War came in Vietnam. Before World War II, part of Indochina (between India and China) had been a French colony. The French unwisely tried to retake it after the war. In Vietnam, they were opposed by Ho Chi Minh, a communist. Minh became very popular in the 1950s as his soldiers fought for the freedom of Vietnam from French domination. Because he was communist, the U.S. provided military aid to the French. In spite of the aid, the communist guerrillas, called Vietminh, continued to defeat the French. In March of 1954, the Vietminh overran a key French fortress called Dien Bien Phu. At that point, the French finally gave up.

An international conference made Laos, Cambodia, and Vietnam independent. Vietnam, however, was divided at the 17th parallel. The communists were given control of the north. The two sides were supposed to be united under free elections within two years. However, the Southern leaders feared the communists would destroy democracy. They, therefore, (with U.S. support) refused to participate. Thus, the U.S. found itself supporting an undemocratic government in the South against a popular leader in the north who had liberated his people from colonial rule. U.S. policy makers saw no alternative if communism was to be contained.

**Thaw?** Nikita Khrushchev arose as the new leader of the U.S.S.R. in the 1950s. He led the Cold War into its first "thaw," a time when the superpowers negotiated their differences and reduced conflict. In 1955 the Soviet Union finally signed a peace treaty with Austria which had also been split into four occupation zones. The treaty allowed that nation to reunite as a free, neutral country.

Khrushchev continued to soften the communist position. He met with President Eisenhower in Geneva, Switzerland later that same year to discuss issues. In 1956 he called for "peaceful coexistence" with the West, which was a big change from Stalin's position that war between the two sides was inevitable. He also denounced Stalin for his brutal excesses. (Stalin had controlled the U.S.S.R. with an iron hand and killed more people than Hitler.)

However, even with the peaceful words, the communist threat never completely withdrew. The U.S.S.R. continued to encourage and finance communist revolts all over the world. It also kept tight control over its European satellites. In 1956 the people of Hungary revolted against their communist leaders. The Soviet Union quickly sent in an army to overthrow the new government and restore communist rule. The leaders of the revolt were executed and about 200,000 people fled to Western Europe. A similar rebellion and bloody reprisal occurred in Czechoslovakia in 1968.

**Middle East**. In 1948 the nation of Israel was reestablished in the Middle East after 1,878 years. The Arab, Islamic nations nearby immediately attacked and were defeated in a series of wars. The conflict between the Arabs and Israel was drawn into the Cold War, usually with the U.S. supporting Israel and the Soviet Union supporting the more aggressive Arab nations. Both of the superpowers tried to expand their influence in this oil-rich region by the use of financial aid.

Egypt in the mid-1950s came under the control of Gamal Abdel Nasser, an Arab nationalist who wanted to unite all Arabs under Egypt. Nasser needed money to build the massive Aswan Dam on the Nile for irrigation and electrical power. The U.S. and Britain offered to fund the project until Nasser began to make contacts with the Soviets. When the West withdrew its offer of aid, Nasser seized the Suez Canal, which was owned by French and British investors, intending to use the passage fees to build the dam. He closed the canal to Israeli traffic and threatened the supply of oil to Europe, which came through the canal.

Britain and France were irate and worked with Israel who was concerned about the expansion of Egyptian power. The nations attacked together in October of 1956. The French and British seized the canal while the Israelis attacked the Sinai Peninsula. America had not been informed of the assault and Eisenhower was furious with his impetuous allies. Under pressure, the three nations agreed to a cease fire, withdrew their troops and allowed U.N.

forces to take over their positions. Eventually, the Soviet Union financed the Aswan Dam for Egypt.

**Eisenhower Doctrine**. Soviet activities in Egypt alarmed the U.S. In 1957 Congress approved the Eisenhower Doctrine which permitted the president to use armed force to assist any nation in the Middle East that asked for help against aggression from a communist nation. The Doctrine was used to support Lebanon in 1958 after a revolution threw out a pro-Western government in nearby Iraq.

 **Choose the correct person.** (Some will be used more than once.)

1.20 _____ leader of Egypt, Arab nationalist

1.21 _____ American general in Korea

1.22 _____ U.S. president at the end of the Korean War

1.23 _____ Vietnamese communist

1.24 _____ leader of the U.S.S.R. in the 1950s

1.25 _____ U.S. president, start of the Korean War

1.26 _____ general fired for insubordination

1.27 _____ Communist victor in China, 1949

1.28 _____ leader of the Nationalist Chinese

1.29 _____ Attacked Stalin for his excesses and called for peaceful coexistence with the West

1.30 _____ took over the Suez Canal to use the income for the Aswan Dam

1.31 _____ fought against the French reconquest of Vietnam after World War II

1.32 _____ President who became very unpopular for a time for firing the U.S. commander in Korea

1.33 _____ Chinese leader that had the support of the huge peasant population

1.34 _____ corrupt Chinese leader, driven out to the island of Taiwan

a. Harry S. Truman

b. Mao Zedong

c. Chiang Kai Shek

d. Douglas MacArthur

e. Nikita Khrushchev

f. Dwight D. Eisenhower

g. Gamal Abdel Nasser

h. Ho Chi Minh

**Give the information requested.**

**1.35** The two events that made 1949 a bad year for the West _____

_____

_____

**1.36** Why the Soviet Union did not veto the protection of South Korea by the U.N. _____

_____

**1.37** The name of the defensive line that held the southeast corner of Korea after the North

attacked in 1950 _____

**1.38** Nation the U.S.S.R. finally allowed to reunite as free country in 1955 _____

_____

**1.39** Issue that stalled the Korean peace talks for two years _____

_____

**1.40** The event that finally convinced the French to pull out of Vietnam _____

_____

**1.41** The result of the Hungarian uprising in 1956 _____

_____

_____

**1.42** MacArthur's solution for advancing back up the Korean Peninsula in Sept. 1950 _____

_____

**1.43** Place where the Korean War stalemated and the demilitarized zone was set up _____

_____

**1.44** Nations that attacked Egypt in 1956 _____

**1.45** The reason why Korea was communist in the north and free in the South _____

_____

_____

**1.46** "Defensive" alliance of the Eastern Bloc _____

**1.47** The Eisenhower Doctrine and where it was used in 1958

a. _____

_____

b. _____

**Technology Race**. A race for technology was also part of the Cold War. Both sides particularly worked to develop new ways to control and deliver atomic weapons. One key advance was the ICBM (intercontinental ballistic missile). These rockets were built to deliver atomic bombs to targets half a world away. Over the years of the Cold War, these self-guided bombs became bigger and more accurate. They were also built into special silos that could survive a nuclear attack and return fire. Elaborate precautions were taken to make sure the missiles could not be destroyed by an enemy's first strike.

The Soviets had one unusual advantage in the atomic race, a society that wasn't free. People had very reasonable fears of nuclear weapons. Americans and Europeans in their free societies openly debated whether the weapons should be built and put in place for use. The Soviets encouraged protests in the West against nuclear weapons. They financed elaborate propaganda that aided anti-nuclear groups in the Free World. Sometimes the protests in the West were loud and widespread, but the Western Bloc pressed ahead and refused to let down their guard. On the other hand, behind the Iron Curtain there were no protests as the governments spent money on nuclear weapons and technology. Protests were not allowed.

**Sputnik**. The Soviet Union shocked the West in October of 1957, by successfully launching the world's first artificial satellite into space, *Sputnik I*. It was followed just a month later by another satellite that carried a small dog. It would be four months after *Sputnik* before the first American satellite, *Explorer I*, was successfully launched into space. The Soviets gloated that their success proved the superiority of their system, as they did every time they beat the West at anything.

Americans were shocked and frightened by the prospect of a Soviet advantage in space and rocketry. The primary fear was that they had also developed more advanced missiles. President Eisenhower reacted by setting up NASA (the National Aeronautics and Space Administration) to coordinate U.S. space exploration and push the U.S. missile program forward.

NASA was an exceptional success. Although starting behind the Soviet space program, NASA quickly caught up and made America the world leader in space exploration. The Soviets put the first man in space and they were the first to have a man orbit the earth (1961). NASA, however, succeeded in putting the first men on the moon (1969) and developed the first reusable space craft, the Space Shuttle (1981). The moon landing in 1969 was a world-wide event that greatly enhanced American prestige. Millions of people watched on their televisions, as American Astronaut Neil Armstrong took the first human steps on the moon, saying "That's one small step for man. One giant leap for mankind." Thus, much of America's spectacular success in space and satellite technology was a product of the Cold War.

**U-2 Affair**. As part of the continuing thaw between the U.S. and the U.S.S.R., Eisenhower invited Khrushchev to visit America in 1959. Khrushchev toured the nation amid a great deal of publicity. However, even in this atmosphere of friendship, he harshly predicted to his American listeners that "your grandchildren will live under communism." He and Eisenhower met for talks at Camp David, the presidential retreat. The talks produced little except that Khrushchev withdrew an ultimatum he made that the West had to evacuate West Berlin. Another summit was scheduled for Paris in May of 1960, and Eisenhower was invited to visit the U.S.S.R. afterward.

The U.S. had been keeping track of Soviet missile development by the use of spy planes. The planes flew at high altitudes over Soviet territory and took pictures of missile and military sites. Just days before the summit was to begin, the Soviets shot down one of the U-2 spy planes and captured the pilot, Francis Gary Powers, alive. At first, the U.S. issued bungling denials about the plane's mission. Eventually, Eisenhower admitted the truth and accepted full responsibility. He refused to apologize, however, or stop the flights. Khrushchev stormed out of the Paris meeting and withdrew his invitation for the president to visit Russia.

**Cuba**. Latin America was suffering from its own woes in the post-war era, mainly from poverty and non-democratic governments. The island of Cuba was an excellent example. From 1933 to 1959 the government was usually under the control of Fulgencio Batista, a dictator. He encouraged American investment in the island, which is only 70 miles south of Florida. As a result, a very wealthy elite of Cubans and Americans ran the nation's economy while most of the people lived in poverty without any political power.

Batista was overthrown in 1959 by a revolutionary named Fidel Castro. At first, the U.S. supported the new regime. However, Castro quickly began to seize American-owned property and relations between the two nations soured. Castro signed a trade agreement with the U.S.S.R. in 1960, so the U.S. stopped buying Cuban sugar. In January, 1961 the U.S. cut off relations with Cuba, by then a communist dictatorship.

| Francis Gary Powers and a U-2 Spyplane

Cuba would be a thorn in the side of the U.S. for many years, even after the fall of communism in Russia. The main problem was the threat of a communist nation that close to the American mainland. Also, Castro's economy depended heavily on money and trade concessions from the Soviets. As a result, he was a willing ally for any "wars of liberation" supported by the U.S.S.R. Cuban troops fought in many communist-sponsored revolts in Latin America and Africa, with the Soviets providing the money and the weapons.

**Bay of Pigs**. There was strong support in the U.S. government for overthrowing Castro. A group of Cubans who fled the island when he came to power planned to do that in 1961. They were trained by the American CIA (Central Intelligence Agency) with the knowledge and support of Eisenhower. President Kennedy allowed the plan to go as scheduled in April of 1961. However, he did not provide the military aid that had been promised and the people of the island did not support the invasion. As a result, the invasion at the Bay of Pigs in Southern Cuba was a disaster. The invaders were quickly killed or captured and the U.S. suffered a very embarrassing blow to its prestige.

**Cuban Missile Crisis**. The Cuban Missile Crisis was possibly the most dangerous event of the Cold War. The two superpowers came perilously close to a direct confrontation over this in 1962. It began in October, when spy pictures revealed that the Soviets were in the process of building missile bases in Cuba. Atomic missiles from those bases could have reached most of the continental United States.

Kennedy could not let those missiles be installed, yet he did not want to start a war. Instead, he established a naval blockade around the island to prevent the missiles from being delivered. He demanded the bases be dismantled. However, the seizure of a Soviet ship coming into Cuba would be likely to trigger a war. The question was whether or not the Soviets would challenge the blockade. The world held its breath while Moscow decided. The ships carrying the missiles turned back, rather than challenge the blockade.

Khrushchev offered to remove the missiles in exchange for a U.S. promise never to invade Cuba. He followed that offer with a demand that the U.S. remove the missiles it had in Turkey in return for removing the bases in Cuba. Kennedy accepted the first offer and ignored the second. The Cuban launch sites were dismantled and the U.S. quietly removed its out-of-date missiles in Turkey several months later.

**Berlin Wall**. Berlin was a sore spot in East-West relations throughout the Cold War. The Western and Eastern sectors had separate governments by 1948, but people could still cross between the two sections freely. Many people fled East Germany by traveling to East Berlin and crossing into the Western sector where they were given asylum.

| The Berlin Wall before 1989

In the late 1950s and early 60s the Soviets kept threatening to turn over control of Berlin's access routes to the East German government. That would have made Berlin hostage to a communist government which was not bound by the Yalta agreements as the Soviets were. The threat was never carried out, but it raised tensions in Europe. Millions of East Germans fled to the west through Berlin.

The government of East Germany was desperate to stop the outflow of people which reached a height of 1,000 people a day. Many of those leaving were talented young people who saw no future for themselves under communism. Very suddenly, on August 13, 1961, Soviet and East German soldiers sealed the border between East and West Berlin. They immediately began to build a wall to enclose the eastern part of the city. Eventually, the Berlin Wall included tank traps, barbed wire, guard towers, attack dogs, and a high concrete fence which separated the two parts of the city. The West Germans called it **Schandmauer** (wall of shame). It would stand until 1989.

**Identify the person, item, or crisis.**

1.48 _____ broke up the Paris summit in 1960

1.49 _____ device used by the communists to stop East Germans from defecting to the West through Berlin

1.50 _____ the Soviet ships carrying missiles turned back rather than challenge an American blockade of Cuba

1.51 _____ a U.S. sponsored invasion of Cuba that failed completely

1.52 _____ Soviet satellite, first ever put into orbit

1.53 _____ American space development group founded by Eisenhower

1.54 _____ dictator of Cuba until 1959

1.55 _____ Communist dictator of Cuba after 1959

1.56 _____ rockets designed to carry atomic bombs halfway around the world

1.57 _____ superpower that sent the first animal and man into space

1.58 _____ superpower that put the first man on the moon and developed the first reusable spacecraft

1.59 _____ threatened Americans that "your grandchildren will live under communism"

1.60 _____ this nation's soldiers used Soviet money and weapons to fight for communism all over the world

1.61 _____ American and Soviet leaders who faced off over missile bases in Cuba in 1961

_____

1.62 _____ European city divided into two parts by the Cold War

1.63 _____ Kennedy promised not to do this to end the crisis over missiles in Cuba

## Vietnam

The war in Vietnam was a major turning point in the Cold War for American policy and self-confidence. The U.S. backed out of the bitter Vietnamese War, which it could not win, leaving an ally to fall to communism. It was a humiliating failure that still scars American thinking.

**Why**. The U.S. became deeply involved in Vietnam for several reasons. American policy makers wanted an option between appeasement and nuclear war to prevent the spread of communism. The use of American soldiers to protect non-communist countries in small, "limited" wars seemed to be a good option. There was a substantial fear that if one nation fell to communism, it would naturally export the "disease" to its neighbors. The entire region would fall like dominoes. The "domino theory" made Americans fearful of losing even a small, unimportant nation to communism. Also, since all communist countries were believed to be loyal to Moscow, there was a fear that communist expansion would build an unshakable Soviet world empire. Thus, the U.S. committed its immense power to prevent South Vietnam from falling to communism.

**Diem's Failure**. The government of South Vietnam had been organized under President Ngo Dinh Diem in 1955, after the Geneva Accords divided the nation in 1954. The U.S. supported Diem when he refused to participate in elections for the entire nation. War began in 1957 when the followers of Ho Chi Minh in South Vietnam began a revolt against Diem's government. The Viet Cong, as they were called, saw this as a continuation of their war for independence. The Viet Cong and the Vietminh (North Vietnamese,) steadily expanded their numbers and attacks in the South. They were kept well-supplied by China and the U.S.S.R. using the Ho Chi Minh trail that ran from North Vietnam through neutral Laos and Cambodia.

| The Vietnam War

The U.S. sent advisors and aid to the Diem's government to protect it from the revolt. Washington initially hoped to support the regime until it could establish a free economy and social justice that would turn the people forever against communism. However, Diem was more interested in his own power than his people. His persecution of Buddhists drew sharp protests from his own people. Finally, Kennedy tacitly approved of a military coup that overthrew Diem, resulting in his death in 1963. By that time, the U.S. had thousands of military and civilian advisors in the South.

The coup destroyed the remaining stability of the South Vietnamese government. Several military governments came to power in the following years. None of them had widespread support among the people. Most were seen as U.S. puppets. In the meantime, the Viet Cong and Vietminh troops took over more and more of the countryside in the South.

**Gulf of Tonkin Incident**. Two U.S. naval destroyers were allegedly attacked by the North Vietnamese in the Gulf of Tonkin in August of 1964. President Johnson seized on the incident as an excuse to use U.S. troops to turn the tide in South Vietnam. He persuaded Congress to authorize him to take whatever measures the president thought were necessary to protect American forces in Southeast Asia. This sweeping Gulf of Tonkin Resolution was the legal basis for sending in U.S. troops without a declaration of war. It was a blank check for the presidents to do as they pleased. After the 1964 elections were over, Johnson sent the first American troops to fight in Vietnam.

The U.S. strategy was to destroy the communist army in the South. The better organized and better equipped Americans consistently won the battles. For years, the U.S. sent more men, weapons, advisors, and aid, but they could never eliminate the enemy. Men and supplies continued to come from the north. U.S. policy would not permit an advance into North Vietnam because that might trigger a war with Russia or China. Instead, the U.S. only bombed the North. At the high point of American involvement in 1969, over 500,000 American soldiers were fighting in the war, handicapped by their inability to attack the enemy at the source of his strength, North Vietnam.

The Viet Cong favored a strategy of guerrilla warfare. They worked in small groups attacking and retreating. They laid ambushes and traps wherever they went. They often retreated into Laos or Cambodia where U.S. troops could not follow because those were neutral nations. The success of these tactics led to a military stalemate in South Vietnam.

**Effect at Home**. In the U.S. by the end of the 1960s, a reaction had set in against the war. Television coverage brought the horrors of war into every living room. The increasing number of dead Americans, and the sheer cost of the war made it very unpopular. War spending caused inflation and forced cutbacks

| The Evacuation of Saigon

in spending on social programs. Many people began to question whether it was worth the cost and why we were supporting the unpopular, corrupt Southern government. Young people who hated the war, staged huge (and often violent) protests that raged across the nation. Young men fled to Canada rather than be drafted to serve in the unpopular war. The many men that did serve honorably found themselves hated and scorned by their own countrymen.

**Tet Offensive**. The U.S. government insisted that it was winning the war. However, in January 1968 the communists launched a major offensive against the Southern cities during the Vietnamese New Year Festival, Tet. The Viet Cong and Vietminh suffered massive casualties as the surprise assault was slowly turned back. However, the attack proved the communists were stronger than the U.S. government had admitted. Americans began to distrust their government even more. As a result, President Johnson cut back the war effort and did not run for reelection in 1968. Peace negotiations were also opened, but they stalled.

**U.S. Withdrawal**. President Nixon, who was elected in 1968, took the Cold War in a new direction. In Vietnam, he began the process he called "Vietnamization." The goal was for the South Vietnamese to take over the fighting while the U.S. slowly withdrew. He pushed secret peace talks which quickly stalled.

Nixon also freely expanded the war to put pressure on the North to negotiate. In 1970 he authorized an attack on communist supply bases in Cambodia. When the peace talks produced an unacceptable agreement in 1972, he ordered bombing resumed in the north. These produced huge protests in America. The nation wanted out of the pointless, endless war.

North and South Vietnam finally agreed to a "cease fire" in January of 1973. U.S. soldiers left by the end of March. However, the peace treaty did not bring peace. It just created a lull in the fighting that allowed the U.S. to get out of the longest and most controversial war in its history. Nixon called it "peace with honor," but there was no peace and no honor, just a retreat under cover of treaty. North Vietnam kept many of its soldiers in the South, and rapidly began new offensives.

The end for South Vietnam came in April of 1975, when the Northern army captured the Southern capital of Saigon. One of the enduring images of the war was the sight of hundreds of Americans and South Vietnamese officials lined up to take helicopters to safety from the top of the U.S. Embassy as the communist army poured into the city. The U.S. Congress refused to send any aid, washing their hands of the whole situation.

Vietnam was reunited, although under a communist government. Thousands of South Vietnamese were sent to "re-education camps," concentration camps where they were mistreated and forced to learn communist ideology. Thousands more risked death in leaky, overcrowded boats in an attempt to flee. The "boat people" filled refugee camps in the nearby nations. Thousands of American lives and billions of U.S. dollars had not prevented the fall of South Vietnam.

**Cambodia**. Cambodia, also called Kampuchea, had also been fighting the communists who were using their nation as a base against South Vietnam. In 1975 a Cambodian communist group called the Khmer Rouge took over the nation. Their leader, Pol Pot, was a follower of Mao Zedong and a believer in continuous revolution. He ordered the cities emptied. Educated people were killed. All of the people were forced to work by hand on farms. Over a million people (perhaps as much as one-fifth of the population) died of mistreatment, disease, hunger or murder. The Khmer Rouge was defeated in 1979 by the Vietnamese who invaded and installed a puppet regime there. Laos had fallen to the communists in 1975, thus the U.S. loss was total in French Indochina.

 **Complete these sentences.**

**1.64** Congress authorized the president to conduct the war in Vietnam by passing the

_____ .

**1.65** The horrors of war became very real to most Americans because of the

_____ coverage.

**1.66** The _____ in January of 1968 proved that the communists were very strong in South Vietnam.

**1.67** _____ was the South Vietnamese leader who was overthrown by a military coup in 1963.

**1.68** The South Vietnamese communists were called the _____ while those from the North were the _____ .

**1.69** Nixon's plan to turn the war over to the South Vietnamese was called _____ _____ .

**1.70** _____ was the leader of the Cambodian communists known as the _____ , who killed over a million people in the mid-1970s.

**1.71** The idea that if one nation became communist, its neighbors would soon do so also was called the _____ theory.

**1.72** The U.S. strategy in the Vietnam War was to _____ _____ _____ in the South without invading _____ .

**1.73** The defeat of South Vietnam was completed in 1975 with the fall of the city of _____ _____ .

**1.74** The communists in Vietnam used _____ warfare.

**1.75** Thousands of South Vietnamese were sent to _____ camps or became _____ attempting to flee after 1975.

**1.76** The North and South signed a _____ in 1973 that allowed the U.S. to _____ .

**1.77** As the war became unpopular, there were widespread _____ in the U.S. against it.

**1.78** Not only Vietnam, but the neighboring nations of _____ and _____ fell to communism in the 1970s.

**Review the material in this section in preparation for the Self Test.** The Self Test will check your mastery of this particular section. The items missed on this Self Test will indicate specific areas where restudy is needed for mastery.

# SELF TEST 1

**Choose the correct person for each description** (2 points, each answer).

**1.01** _____ Leader of Egypt, took over the Suez
Canal to pay for the Aswan Dam

**1.02** _____ Set up containment as U.S. policy

**1.03** _____ Created a communist dictatorship in Cuba

**1.04** _____ Leader of the U.S.S.R. in the 1950s

**1.05** _____ Nationalist Chinese leader, fled to Taiwan

**1.06** _____ South Vietnamese leader, refused to allow
elections with the North, overthrown and
killed by a military coup

**1.07** _____ American commander in Korea, fired
for insubordination

**1.08** _____ Communist victor in China, believed in
continuous revolution

**1.09** _____ Cambodian communist, killed over a million
people due to his ideas on revolution

**1.010** _____ Pro-American Cuban dictator overthrown by a revolution in 1959

**1.011** _____ Communist leader of North Vietnam, fought the French and Americans

a. Harry S. Truman

b. Ho Chi Minh

c. Mao Zedong

d. Chiang Kai Shek

e. Nikita Khrushchev

f. Douglas MacArthur

g. Gamal Abdel Nasser

h. Fidel Castro

i. Fulgencio Batista

j. Ngo Dinh Diem

k. Pol Pot

**Answer these questions** (each answer, 5 points).

**1.012** What was the Cold War and what kept it from becoming "hot?" _____

_____

_____

_____

**1.013** What was the Containment Policy and how was it enforced? _____

_____

_____

_____

**Choose the correct letter** (each answer, 2 points).

1.014 _____ American space agency created to catch up with the Soviets in rocketry and space explorations

1.015 _____ North Vietnamese attack during New Year, showed they were not as weak as U.S. claimed

1.016 _____ South Vietnamese communists

1.017 _____ America's first permanent alliance since the 1770s, to protect against communism

1.018 _____ Could deliver nuclear bombs half a world away

1.019 _____ First artificial satellite, Soviet

1.020 _____ Failed attempt to overthrow Castro

1.021 _____ New policy of U.S.S.R. toward the U.S. after the death of Stalin

1.022 _____ "Defensive" alliance of the communist nations

1.023 _____ Name for the Free or First World

1.024 _____ Dividing line between the free and communist nations of Europe

1.025 _____ A war fought to stop communism in a specific country that was not allowed to spread

1.026 _____ Supplied the divided German capital for a year when the Soviets blockaded it, 1948-49

1.027 _____ U.S. blockaded Castro's island to prevent the delivery of Soviet missiles, Soviets backed down

1.028 _____ U.S. would assist any nation in the Middle East that wanted aid against communist aggression

1.029 _____ Aid to Europe that helped it recover from World War II

1.030 _____ New postwar league of nations which the U.S. quickly joined

1.031 _____ Communist Bloc or the Second World nations

1.032 _____ Congress gave the president uncontrolled freedom to use force in Vietnam

1.033 _____ Undeveloped nations, not closely allied with any side in the Cold War

1.034 _____ Way to stop East Germans from escaping to the West through Berlin

1.035 _____ An American spy plane was shot down over Russia and the pilot captured, ended plans for a summit and Eisenhower's visit to the U.S.S.R

a. United Nations
b. Marshall Plan
c. Iron Curtain
d. Berlin Airlift
e. NATO
f. Sputnik
g. NASA
h. peaceful coexistence
i. Eisenhower Doctrine
j. U-2 Affair
k. ICBM
l. Bay of Pigs
m. Cuban Missile Crisis
n. Berlin Wall
o. Gulf of Tonkin Resolution
p. Tet Offensive
q. limited war
r. Viet Cong
s. Third World
t. Warsaw Pact
u. Eastern Bloc
v. Western Bloc

**Answer these questions** (each answer, 5 points).

**1.036**  What was the course of the fighting in the Korean War? _____

_____

_____

_____

_____

**1.037**  What issue held up the peace talks in the Korean War and how was it resolved? _____

_____

_____

_____

_____

**1.038**  Why was the war in Vietnam unpopular and how did many Americans react to it? _____

_____

_____

_____

_____

**1.039**  What Soviet actions after World War II started the Cold War? _____

_____

_____

_____

**Answer this question** (4 points).

**1.040**  Why was 1949 a bad year for the West? _____

_____

_____

_____

| 80 / 100 | | SCORE _____ | TEACHER _____ _____ |
| --- | --- | --- | --- |
| | | | initials        date |

# 2. BETWEEN WAR AND WATERGATE

America went through many conflicts between World War II, and the scandal called "Watergate" in the 1970s. The era of the Korean War saw the national government torn apart by unjust searches for American communists. Black Americans rose up and organized to demand their rights as citizens. They were violently opposed by some deeply prejudiced white Americans. A president, a famous black leader, and a presidential candidate died by assassination. Young people staged a mass, public rebellion against the values and ideals of American society.

The unpopular Vietnamese War pitted Americans against each other. The Cold War entered a new thaw when the U.S restored relations with China, and signed several agreements with the U.S.S.R. These, however, did not resolve the fundamental conflict. Finally, a president was forced to resign after a two-year long scandal which dragged his office to its lowest place in generations. In the last section, it was shown that there was trauma abroad. This section will show how the post-war years were very traumatic for America at <u>home</u>.

## SECTION OBJECTIVES

**Review these objectives**. When you have completed this section, you should be able to:

1.  Describe the course of the Cold War and the incidents within it.
2.  Name the presidents of the Cold War and the events that happened during their administration.
3.  Describe the course of the Civil Rights Movement.
4.  Describe events in America and changes in American thinking during the Cold War era.
5.  Name the important people on both sides of the Cold War.

## VOCABULARY

**Study these words to enhance your learning success in this section**.

**censure** (sen' chər). A judgment involving condemnation.

**conventional** (kən vench' nəl). Not making use of nuclear powers.

**détente** (dā tänt). A relaxation of strained relations or tensions between nations.

**inflation** (in flā' shən). A substantial and continuing rise in the general level of prices.

**poll** (pōl). A questioning or canvassing of persons selected at random or by quota to obtain information or opinions to be analyzed.

**subpoena** (sə pē nə). A writ commanding a person designated in it to appear in court under a penalty for failure.

## Truman/Eisenhower

**Post-war economy**. Truman had to deal with the problems created by the end of World War II as well as the Cold War. After years of crisis (the Great Depression and the war) no one was certain how the American economy would react in the 1940s. The two biggest fears were a depression when war spending stopped, or massive **inflation** as people spent their war savings. There was also a housing shortage because building supplies were not available during the war.

A depression was never a serious threat. During the war, people had earned large amounts of money which they could not spend, because consumer goods were not available. After 1945, the manufacturers quickly retooled to produce those goods, creating jobs. People quickly started buying, keeping the manufacturing going. A boom in construction, especially homes, also created jobs. The G.I. Bill of Rights (passed in 1944) gave veterans loans, grants for college, and other benefits that helped them adjust to civilian life.

Inflation, however, quickly became a problem after the war. Truman wanted to continue the price controls implemented during the war, but the Republican Congress elected in 1946 did not. Price controls were weakened and then eliminated by the end of 1946. Prices continued to rise rapidly, but wages did not go up as fast. The result was widespread labor disputes and strikes.

Truman wanted to continue and expand F.D.R.'s liberal programs. His proposals included a national health care system, civil rights legislation, expansion of Social Security, and laws to protect minorities in employment. The Congress enacted only a fair employment act, giving Truman fodder for the 1948 presidential election. The Republican Congress, however, did pass the Taft-Hartley act that restricted the power of unions, over Truman's veto.

| Truman defeated Dewey in 1948.

**Election of 1948**. The Democratic Party split three ways in 1948. A group of liberal Democrats formed a new Progressive Party around nominee Henry Wallace favoring a more conciliatory attitude toward the Soviets. Truman was selected as the nominee for the Democratic Party at its convention. However, the party platform called for civil rights legislation to fight discrimination against blacks. Southern Democrats walked out and nominated their own candidate, Strom Thurmond of South Carolina, calling themselves the States' Rights or "Dixiecrat" Party.

The delighted Republicans had every reason to believe they would have an easy victory. They renominated Thomas E. Dewey who had lost to Roosevelt in 1944. Dewey, however, was dangerously overconfident, especially after he established a big lead in the **polls**. He did not establish any clear-cut proposals; in fact, he was deliberately vague about everything.

Truman, on the other hand, surprised everyone. He set out on the road to make a fight of it. He toured the country by train, making speeches at all the stops. He attacked the "do nothing" Congress. He lambasted the Taft-Hartley Act and swung hard at his opponents on every front. His common touch and hard fighting attitude rapidly won support. In the end, he beat out Dewey and both of his quasi-Democratic opponents.

**Fair Deal**. The Democrats won control of Congress in 1948, which gave Truman high hopes for his legislative program called the "Fair Deal." It was an ambitious expansion of the New Deal. Opposed by conservative Democrats, the program was not very successful. Congress, however, did pass an increase in the minimum wage, an expansion of Social Security, some public works projects, and some low-income housing. Truman's civil rights program, national health insurance, and agricultural reforms, however, all failed.

**Bad Deal**. The tensions with the U.S.S.R. produced an avalanche of anti-communist sympathy in the U.S. The Cold War crisis made people fearful that they might lose their freedoms to this odious system. Their fears were directed not only against the Soviets, but also against real or imagined communist agents in America. People believed the accusations that communists in the federal government were working to destroy the nation.

These fears were reinforced by two prominent cases. The first case involved Alger Hiss, who had been a prominent official in the State Department. He was credibly accused of having passed secrets to a communist spy. The spy, Whittaker Chambers, changed sides and denounced him in 1948. He produced enough evidence for Hiss to be convicted of perjury for denying the charge under oath. The second case involved Julius and Ethel Rosenberg. They were convicted in 1951 of sending atomic bomb secrets to the Soviet Union. They were executed amidst great controversy in 1953.

In this atmosphere, Truman set up the Federal Employee Loyalty Program, which investigated federal workers. Congress set up its own committees to do the same thing. The committees' investigations resulted in few criminal charges, but also led to a great deal of harassment and intimidation. Hundreds of government, media, and university employees lost their jobs because they favored communism, did not favor strong opposition to communism, had communist/socialist friends or were simply too stubborn to answer questions they felt violated their rights.

**Election of 1952**. Truman chose not to run in 1952 and gave his support to the Democratic nominee, Adlai Stevenson, governor of Illinois. The Republicans, however, gained the upper hand by nominating the incredibly popular war hero, Dwight (Ike) Eisenhower. Senator Richard M. Nixon from California, a virulent anti-communist, was chosen as his running mate.

The Republican campaign centered on the popularity of their candidate. The campaign slogan said it all: "I Like Ike." Nixon attacked the Democrats as soft on communism, while Ike dramatically promised to personally go to Korea and end that war. During the campaign, it came out that Nixon had access to a secret fund set up in California for his political expenses. Nixon defended himself in an emotional speech and was kept on the ticket by Eisenhower. They won an easy victory and the Republicans gained control of the House and a tie in the Senate.

**Dwight D. Eisenhower (1890-1969)**. Dwight David Eisenhower was very popular and successful, both as a general and as president. He was born in Denison, Texas and grew up in Abilene, Kansas. His father worked in a creamery, and from an early age, Dwight did odd jobs to help support the family. After high school, he worked one year to support a brother in college and, then, secured an appointment to West Point, where he could get a college education paid for by the tax payers.

After graduation in 1915, he served in various posts all over the world. He trained recruits in the U.S. during World War I. Eventually, he impressed his superiors enough that he was given special training for leadership within the army. When World War II came, he was selected to command the U.S. forces for invasion of North Africa and, later, all Allied forces in Europe. He showed considerable skill in making all of the different Allied armies and their opinionated commanders work together. He was eventually promoted to the newly- created rank of five star general. After the war, he served as Army Chief of Staff. He retired briefly to become the president of Columbia University and was recalled to duty to serve as the first commander of NATO. He retired from that to run for the presidency in 1952.

**McCarthy**. The most famous of the anti-communist Congressmen was Senator Joseph McCarthy of Wisconsin. He became an incredibly powerful person for several years before 1954. His technique was accusing people of being communists in the State Department, or some other organization. He could never prove his charges, but it did not matter. People believed him. He ruined the careers of many honest men by denouncing them as communists on little or no evidence. He did considerable damage to the morale and effectiveness of the government in the early 1950s. People were afraid of him.

McCarthy's witch hunt led him to attack the army in 1954. However, the end of the Korean War in 1953 had eased Cold War tensions and the army fought back. Senate hearings on McCarthy's charges were shown live on television. In the hearings, McCarthy finally came across as a lying bully tossing around unproven charges. He lost public support, was **censured** by the Senate, and faded into obscurity. His excesses made "McCarthyism" a name for an unfair, intrusive investigation based on questionable or made up evidence.

**Civil Rights–Background**. The Civil War had settled the issue of slavery, but had left black Americans as second-class citizens. They were forced to use segregated, inferior public facilities, and schools. They were often denied the right to vote by special laws or intimidation. They were discriminated against in employment, housing, and services. However, by the 1950s American attitudes were finally beginning to change, and African-Americans began an effective campaign to receive equal treatment under the law.

Violent opposition to black equality in the South, and more passive acceptance of white superiority in the North, had kept African-Americans from acting sooner. Black leaders of the post-Civil War era faced immense cultural pressure for blacks to accept an inferior position. The greatest black leader of the post-Civil War era, Booker T. Washington, was an excellent example of this dilemma.

Washington was born into slavery, but managed by hard work to obtain an education and, eventually, a nationwide reputation as an educator and spokesman for African-Americans. He founded and led Tuskegee Institute, which taught black students trades such as carpentry. Faced with the general ignorance of most blacks, who had just recently escaped slavery, and the violent hostility of whites, who held all the political power, Washington argued for a slow approach to black equality. He urged blacks to learn a trade and make themselves successful in the American economy. He accepted segregation as a temporary measure to allow black Americans time to build up their wealth and level of education. He stressed the need for blacks to get along with the system for now and wait until they became more economically successful before demanding legal equality.

Washington saw his plan as a slow path to equality. Many white people supported it because it had the effect of keeping black Americans "in their place." Washington's chief opponent was W.E.B. DuBois, a black historian, sociologist, and communist party member. He argued that blacks should have the opportunity for higher education and should press for equality now. DuBois was among the founders of the National Association for the Advancement of Colored People (NAACP), which has historically been in the forefront of the battle for civil rights. At that time, there was almost no public support for black equality.

African-American soldiers fought bravely in both World Wars in segregated units, although they were often assigned to do manual labor rather than fight. In 1948 Truman used his authority to order the federal bureaucracy and the army to integrate. The integrated units did well in Korea in spite of the dire predictions by white supremacists that they would fail. However, Truman had been unable to get civil rights legislation, and Eisenhower did not make it a priority. Finally, however, the African-Americans and the courts stepped in and got the ball rolling.

**Civil Rights–Beginnings**. The modern movement for civil rights began in December of 1955 in Montgomery, Alabama. It was triggered by a black woman named Rosa Parks who refused, one day, to sit in the back of the bus as segregation laws required. She was arrested and the black people of Montgomery rose to support her. Led by Martin Luther King, Jr., a Baptist pastor, they peacefully boycotted the bus system for a year. With the help of the courts, who sided with the protesters, bus segregation in that city was ended. This incident gave Dr. King a national reputation and set off a mass movement among African-Americans to press for full and fair equality.

They were aided in their quest by the federal court system under Earl Warren, Chief Justice of the Supreme Court. The Warren Court moved American law substantially in the direction of individual rights. In 1896 the Supreme Court had ruled in *Plessy v. Ferguson,* that "separate but equal" facilities for blacks and whites were

| Black Student Entering Central High School

constitutional. The facilities had since then been separate, but <u>never</u> equal. The Court reversed itself in *Brown v. Board of Education of Topeka* in 1954. The Court ruled that segregation in education was "inherently unequal" and ordered schools to integrate with "all deliberate speed."

Following a court order, Central High School in Little Rock, Arkansas prepared to admit nine African-American teenagers in 1957. The governor of the state, Orville E. Faubus, mobilized the National Guard and public opinion to stop it. Angry mobs surrounded the school and made it unsafe for the black students to attend. Eisenhower, who had shown little interest in pushing integration, would not let such a challenge to federal authority pass. He sent in armed paratroopers who surrounded the school and escorted the students to class. The image of quiet black students trying to get an education, passing through crowds of jeering, hateful white people began to open the long-closed doors of the American conscience.

In that same year, congress finally passed a new Civil Rights Law (the first since the 1870s). It set up a Civil Rights Commission to investigate violations of the rights of minorities and authorized some protection of voting rights. It was a start, but it lacked the force needed to be effective.

**Second Administration**. Eisenhower easily won reelection in 1956 despite the fact of a heart attack in 1955 and an attack of intestinal problems that required surgery in 1956. Besides civil rights legislation, Eisenhower had several successes during his term. He believed in careful control of government finances. He balanced the federal budget three of his eight years by laying off federal workers and eliminating projects. He did, however, approve several expensive projects that benefitted the nation. He supported a plan to invest billions in an interstate highway system and signed a bill setting up the St. Lawrence Seaway that brought ocean traffic into the Great Lakes.

Eisenhower's personal popularity did not extend to the whole Republican Party, however. The Democrats gained control of Congress in 1954 and kept it through the remainder of Ike's term. Nevertheless, he kept the nation on a steady path of increasing prosperity that was only briefly interrupted by a recession in 1957-58. His legacy was a time of stability and growth—a welcome relief after the tempestuous years leading up to the 1950s.

**Name the item, event, or person.**

2.1 _____ Truman's legislative program

2.2 _____ Anti-communist senator, censured for his accusations

2.3 _____ Post-Civil War black leader, accepted segregation until blacks could gain economic power

2.4 _____ Economic problem right after World War II

2.5 _____ Former State Department official convicted of perjury for lying about passing information to a spy

2.6 _____ First commander of NATO

2.7 _____ The three parties the Democrats split into in 1948
_____
_____

2.8 _____ Anti-union law passed by Republican Congress over Truman's veto

2.9 _____ Set up by Truman to look for government communists
_____

2.10 _____ 1952 Republican presidential slogan

2.11 _____ Black historian/sociologist, helped found NAACP

**2.12** _____     Woman whose decision to sit in front triggered the Civil Rights movement

**2.13** _____     City that Eisenhower sent paratroopers to escort black teenagers to school

**2.14** _____     Gave veterans loans and grants to adjust after the war

**2.15** _____     Supreme Court Chief Justice, expanded individual rights

**2.16** _____     Expensive transportation plans set up under Eisenhower

_____

**2.17** _____     Eisenhower's vice president

**2.18** _____     Court decision ordered the end of segregated education

**2.19** _____     Black pastor who led the Montgomery bus boycott

**2.20** _____     Pair executed for giving atomic secrets to the U.S.S.R.

_____

**2.21** _____     Court decision, allowed "separate but equal"

**Answer these questions.**

**2.22** Who was expected to win the presidency in 1948 and why didn't he? _____

_____

_____

_____

**2.23** What legislation did Truman want that never became laws? _____

_____

_____

_____

## Kennedy/Johnson

**Election of 1960**. The new 22nd Amendment to the Constitution prevented Eisenhower from running in 1960. The Republicans, therefore, nominated Richard Nixon. The Democrats, after a bruising primary fight, selected Senator John F. Kennedy, a Massachusetts millionaire. His closest rival in the party, Senator Lyndon Johnson of Texas, was picked as the vice presidential candidate.

Kennedy was a Roman Catholic and prejudice was still strong enough to be a factor in the campaign. Kennedy won points by facing the issue squarely and assuring Americans that the Pope would not be running the country. Nixon emphasized his own long experience, but the Democrats attacked the easygoing "do nothing" Eisenhower style. The key to the election was probably a series of four televised debates between the candidates (the first in history). The youthful, good-looking Kennedy came across better on TV than Nixon. Kennedy won the election by a thin popular (about 120,000 votes out of 68 million), but comfortable electoral vote (303 to 219). Congress fell to the Democrats by a wide margin.

**John F. Kennedy (1917-1963).** John F. Kennedy has grown into a legend in U.S. history because of his youth, vigor, and sudden death by assassination. John, or "Jack" as he was also known, was the second of eight children born to Joseph and Rose Kennedy. He was born near Boston in 1917. His father was a self-made millionaire whose family was politically active. Jack attended various schools before graduating from Harvard University in 1939. He turned his senior thesis (why Britain had not been ready for war) into a best-selling book.

Kennedy fought in World War II as the commander of a PT boat in the South Pacific. His boat was cut in half by a Japanese destroyer in 1943. Kennedy, suffering from an injured back, towed another injured man to safety on a nearby island. He spent several days searching

| A Peace Corps Volunteer in Africa

for help. Thanks to his efforts, the survivors were rescued five days later. Kennedy received the Navy and Marine Corps Medal for his leadership and heroism.

Jack's older brother, Joseph, was expected to go into politics, but he died in World War II. So, Jack took up the family passion. He served three terms in the U.S. House, beginning in 1946, and defeated a popular long-term Republican senator in 1952. He wrote a Pulitzer Prize winning book, *Profiles in Courage*, during his first term in the Senate, while recovering from surgery for his old back injury. He was re-elected to the Senate in 1958 and successfully ran for president in 1960. His poise and good looks on television helped overcome a perception that he was too young at 43 to take on the responsibilities of the presidency.

**New Frontier**. Kennedy brought a new style into the White House. He and his cabinet were younger than any of his predecessors, and far less passive in their politics. Even Kennedy's family was young. He had a 3 year old daughter, Caroline, and a newborn son, John, Jr., when he was inaugurated. He and his stylish wife, Jackie, were widely admired and emulated. Life in Washington was more active and activist than it had been in years. Kennedy challenged Americans to "ask not what your country can do for you: ask what you can do for your country."

Kennedy called his legislative program the "New Frontier." The Democrats controlled Congress, but the Southern Democrats and Republicans worked together to thwart his agenda, as they had the two previous administrations. The president could not get laws to aid education or mass transportation. He also failed to get a medical insurance for the elderly and a new department for housing and cities. However, he did achieve an increase in the minimum wage, expanded presidential power over tariffs, and some aid for depressed areas, but much of his most ambitious plans stayed snarled up in Congressional committees.

Kennedy's greatest success was the Peace Corps. He started it in 1961 by a presidential order. It was a program to send volunteers to Third World nations to help them improve their living conditions. Corps volunteers worked to improve health care, agriculture, transportation, and housing. These volunteers continue to work all over the world bringing their knowledge and their nation's goodwill.

**Foreign Affairs**. The Cold War pressed hard on the young president. He had to deal with the Bay of Pigs, Soviet threats to give East Germany control of Berlin's supply routes, the Cuban Missile Crisis, and the building of the Berlin Wall during his short administration. Kennedy began a program of aid called the *Alliance for Progress* to promote social reforms in Latin America to reduce the popularity of communism there. He also built up American **conventional** forces to give the U.S. more flexibility than just nuclear weapons. During his term, the U.S. signed a treaty banning atomic bomb testing in the atmosphere, outer space, and under water. This treaty between the U.S., U.S.S.R.,

| Martin Luther King, Jr.

and Britain limited testing to underground, thus eliminating the danger of radioactive fallout. The U.S. and U.S.S.R. also established a "hotline," a direct communications link between the White House and the Kremlin. That gave them immediate access to each other in the event of a crisis. Thus, the trend toward "thaws" continued under Kennedy.

**Civil Rights Movement**. Following the success of the Montgomery bus boycott, Martin Luther King became the center of a nationwide movement for civil rights. King used non-violent protests to fight the segregation that still dominated the South. His firm commitment to peaceful protest and Christian love won widespread support and sympathy, even among white Americans. He rapidly became the most famous and influential African-American in U.S. history.

The movement took off in the 1960s. Young black students stayed at lunch counters when they were refused service. They just sat there, peacefully, blocking the tables. These "sit-ins" spread all over the South. Other protesters "sat-in" on segregated buses, "waded-in" at segregated beaches, and "prayed-in" at segregated churches. The pressure for change mounted quickly.

In 1963 King and his Southern Christian Leadership Conference organized a series of mass demonstrations and marches in Birmingham, Alabama to protest the heavy segregation there. Birmingham police responded by using fire hoses, attack dogs, and cattle prods against the unarmed, peaceful protesters. The entire travesty was captured on national television. It caused an outcry against segregation and prompted Kennedy to propose a stronger civil rights law.

Later that same year, King organized a massive march in Washington D.C. to push for the Civil Rights Act and draw attention to the need for racial equality. The March on Washington drew over 200,000 people to the Lincoln Memorial in August of 1963. There King gave a memorable, stirring speech that called for a color-blind nation. "I Have a Dream" was a challenge to all Americans to fulfill the promise of freedom.

**Kennedy's Death**. On November 22, 1963 Kennedy visited Dallas, Texas. While riding in an open car, he was shot in the head with a rifle from a nearby building. He died moments later at a local hospital. Harvey Oswald, a communist sympathizer, was arrested later that day and charged with the crime. Two days later, Oswald was being moved to another jail when another man, Jack Ruby, shot him. The shooting was seen on national television. The entire episode was so bizarre that a special investigation was conducted under Chief Justice Earl Warren. The Warren Commission decided the evidence showed that Oswald acted alone, but many people still believe theories of some sort of conspiracy.

**Lyndon B. Johnson (1908-1973)**. Lyndon Baines Johnson was sworn in as the nation's 36th president on an airplane carrying

| Johnson and the Expansion of the War in Vietnam

Kennedy's body back to Washington. Johnson was born and raised in central Texas. His parents were teachers who also farmed. He attended local schools and worked his way through Southwest Texas State Teachers College, graduating in 1930. He was successful in debates and school politics in college.

After graduating, Johnson went to Washington as a congressional secretary. In 1935 he was appointed by F.D.R. to run a New Deal administration in Texas. He was elected to the House of Representatives in 1937. During World War II, he served in the navy as a special representative of the president. He was elected to the U.S. Senate in 1948 and 1954, serving as the Democratic majority leader.

Johnson was a remarkable legislator, skilled in the art of passing or preventing laws and getting votes. One of his first acts as president was to push through much of Kennedy's stalled legislation. The Civil Rights Act was passed in 1964. It forbade segregation in public accommodations, barred federal funds for segregated projects, and expanded federal protection of voting rights. He also pushed through a tax cut Kennedy requested and other stalled New Frontier laws.

**Election of 1964**. Johnson easily won the Democratic nomination in 1964. His liberal program, called the Great Society, called for government spending to end poverty in America. His Republican opponent was Senator Barry Goldwater of Arizona, a strong conservative who wanted to undo much of the New Deal. Goldwater was bluntly honest about his beliefs. The Democrats attacked him as unstable and likely to start World War III. The popularity of Johnson's programs and fears about what Goldwater might do gave Johnson a huge victory. He won 43 million votes to Goldwater's 27 million.

**Great Society**. The Congress elected in 1964 had a huge Democratic majority and it proceeded to give Johnson anything he wanted. The deficit soared as money was spent on the War on Poverty, aid to education, medical insurance for the elderly (Medicare), and medical care for the poor (Medicaid). Two new cabinet posts were set up for Housing and Urban Development and Transportation.

Johnson was also the president who expanded the U.S. role in Vietnam. He obtained the Gulf of Tonkin Resolution and used it to commit more and more soldiers to the war. As it dragged on, without an end in sight, protests spread all over the country. War costs forced Congress to cut back spending on the Great Society. Johnson became increasingly unpopular as people began to doubt his war strategy and his honesty about the situation. Finally, the Tet Offensive and a stunning showing by a Democratic opponent in the first 1968 primary, convinced Johnson he was finished. He announced he would not run again.

**Civil Rights Movement**. After the Civil Rights Act, Martin Luther King, Jr. shifted his emphasis to registering black voters. Unjust voting laws, and threats kept many black Americans from voting across the South. A drive to register blacks in Mississippi in 1964 was largely unsuccessful due to violence against the organizers. In 1965 King tried again in Selma, Alabama. State police broke up a peaceful march on the capital with tear gas and whips. Again, the nation was shaken by the violence which was covered by television. Johnson rose to the occasion and quickly passed the Voting Rights Act of 1965 which ended literacy tests (used only to stop black voters) and set up federal registration of voters in several Southern states.

The success of the Civil Rights Movement led to high expectations and anger over slow solutions. Riots broke out in 1965 in Watts, a black section of Los Angeles. Other race riots followed, all over the nation in the next few years. Violence against Civil Rights workers continued, and many black people began to believe that King's non-violent approach was inadequate. Anti-white "Black Power" advocates began to call for violence and some occurred. The Civil Rights Movement lost much of its strength and white support. The riots and the violence by more radical blacks frightened the white majority and took away the movement's high moral standing.

Martin Luther King, Jr. continued to call for peaceful pressure, but in April of 1968 the growing violence of the nation swept over him. He was killed by an assassin's bullet. Riots broke out all over the nation when the news was announced. A white escaped convict named James Earl Ray pled guilty to the shooting and was sentenced to 99 years in jail. As with Kennedy, many people have never accepted the official finding that the assassin acted alone.

The Civil Rights Movement was an amazing success. It forced the end of a hundred years of legal inequality in the "land of the free and the brave." It enabled many talented black artists, teachers, thinkers, and businessmen to fulfill their potential. It promoted black Americans into the halls of power in city, state, and federal governments. Personal prejudice and differences in wealth did and still do exist. The steps taken from 1955 to 1968 were mighty ones, ones that should make all Americans proud of the results and ashamed that it took so long.

**Locate a copy of Dr. Martin Luther King Jr.'s "I Have a Dream" speech, either on-line or in a reference book.** Answer these questions about the speech.

**2.24** How did Dr. King want his children to be judged? _____
_____

**2.25** What patriotic song did he quote? _____
_____

**2.26** What documents wrote the check Dr. King wanted to cash? _____
_____

**2.27** What did he want the sons of former slave owners and slaves to do? _____
_____

**2.28** What did he caution black Americans not to do? _____
_____

**2.29** What is your personal opinion of the speech? _____
_____
_____
_____
_____

**Complete these sentences.**

**2.30** President _____ received his college degree from Southwest Texas Teacher's College.

**2.31** Kennedy wrote a Pulitzer Prize winning book, _____ , while a senator.

**2.32** Kennedy's legislative program was called _____ while Johnson's was _____ .

**2.33** Kennedy probably won the 1960 election because he came across well in _____ _____ .

**2.34** The unpopularity of the _____ forced Johnson not to run for president in 1968.

**2.35** Martin Luther King used _____ protests to push for desegregation.

**2.36** _____ was assassinated in April of 1968 by _____

_____ , an escaped convict.

**2.37** _____ was assassinated on November 22, 1963 in Dallas,

Texas by _____ .

**2.38** The _____ , started by Kennedy, sends volunteers all over the

world to aid developing nations.

**2.39** Lyndon Johnson was a very skilled _____ who was able to

push through much of Kennedy's agenda after his death.

**2.40** Kennedy's aid program to Latin America was called the _____

_____ .

**2.41** King gave his famous _____ speech in Wash-

ington in 1963.

**2.42** Kennedy was a decorated war hero as the commander of a _____

in the South Pacific.

**2.43** The Civil Rights Act of 1964 was proposed after _____

and passed after the assassination of _____ .

**2.44** Kennedy contributed to the Cold War thaw by signing a treaty banning nuclear testing in

_____

and by establishing a communication _____ between Wash-

ington and Moscow

**2.45** At a "sit-in" at a segregated restaurant, Civil Rights protesters would _____

_____ .

**2.46** The Republican candidate in 1960 was _____ and in

1964 it was _____ .

**2.47** A riot in _____ in 1965 was the first

of many across the nation over the next few years.

## Nixon

**Election of 1968**. The 1968 campaign was marred by the violence of the times. Robert Kennedy, brother of the late president, was assassinated in June while campaigning in California. That took away the leading Democratic anti-war candidate. The eventual nominee, Vice President Hubert Humphrey, fully supported the way Johnson had conducted the war. Frustrated anti-war protesters descended on Chicago for the Democratic convention in August. They clashed with police around the convention hall creating a battle zone that television displayed all over the nation. In the meantime, the Republicans nominated Richard Nixon. George C. Wallace of Alabama ran a third party challenge (American Independent Party). Nixon won by a narrow margin, but Congress remained Democratic.

**Richard M. Nixon (1913-1994)**. Richard Milhous Nixon was the only U.S. president ever to resign from office. Nixon was born and raised in California. His father worked at a variety of jobs as did Richard growing up. He graduated from Whittier College (a Quaker school) in 1934 and obtained a law degree from Duke University in 1937. He practiced law in California after graduating and joined the Board of Trustees at Whittier College. He served in the navy during World War II, and two terms in the U.S. House afterward. He was elected to the Senate in 1950, but he left to become vice president under Eisenhower after the 1952 election.

**Social Changes**. The 1960s and early '70s were a time of unrest and change in America. Masses of young people rebelled against the morals and traditions of their parents. They protested *en masse* for and against a variety of causes (drugs, feminism, Vietnam, pollution, college courses, etc.). Marriage and traditional families were rejected. Drug use rose. Some people refused to pursue careers, seeking to live without the bonds of the "money-seeking society" they hated. Many dropped out of

| "Hippies"

society forming bands of "hippies" who claimed to practice universal peace and brotherhood, sharing all that they owned with each other.

The rebellion slowly died as the young adults grew up, facing the responsibilities of children, and the necessity of working to survive. However, they sowed rebellion and we still reap the results. The divorce rate in America had been small in the 1950s, but by the 1990s, half of all marriages ended in divorce. Drug use spread from the inner cities to middle class America. Illegitimacy rose and those children were far more likely to live in poverty. Moral standards in America have fallen steadily since the 1960s. Immorality has become protected by law as in *Roe v. Wade* (1973) that legalized abortion and recent laws allowing doctors to help patients commit suicide. The mass rebellion of the 1960s was the father of the social problems of the 1990s.

**Domestic Issues**. Nixon's main domestic problems were inflation, the Supreme Court and social unrest. Inflation rose in the 1970s. Prices doubled between 1970 and 1980. Without rapid increases in their wages, people actually earned less as the money they made was worth less! The new president tried to slow down the economy and balance the budget by cutting government spending. This caused unemployment without slowing the inflation at all. (This combination of a stagnant economy and inflation was called "stagflation.") He stopped trying to balance the budget and deficits continued to rise. Nixon did not like price controls, but in 1971, under his New Economic Policy, he instituted some. He began with a three month freeze on all wages and prices. He also established boards to regulate salaries and prices, but the efforts were largely ineffective.

The Supreme Court had been very active under Chief Justice Earl Warren. It had expanded the rights of prisoners, banned prayer in schools, and required equal representation in Congressional districts. The Court was very controversial and Nixon had vowed to tame it. He appointed Warren Burger, a conservative judge, to replace Earl Warren in 1969. He was also able to replace three other justices with more conservative men. The new court did not throw out the Warren Court decisions (as Nixon wanted), but it did modify or soften some of them.

The Burger Court continued to be an activist in some areas including school integration. In the early 1970s, the court ordered "busing" to force racial balance for all schools in a district. For example, if most of the white population in a town was in the East and most of the blacks in the West, the Eastern schools would be mainly white and the Western mainly black. Busing required students to be bused to a school across town to obtain the same racial balance in each school. Many people had bought houses near a specific school so their children could go there. Now the children had to ride a bus all the way across town to a different school. Busing was expensive and incredibly unpopular, especially among white Americans. However, it continued in many places until the mid-1980s.

The youthful protesters of the 1960s and early '70s chose the Vietnam War as their favorite cause. These protests reached their height in early '70s as Nixon continued bombing and attacked Cambodia before ending the war. The protests often became violent as students (protests were often at colleges) threw debris, smashed windows, and set fires. At one point, protesters tried to shut down Washington by blocking roads and bridges. One of the worst incidents occurred at Kent State University in May of 1970. National Guardsmen trying to keep order during a protest opened fire on the students. Four people were killed and others wounded.

**Vietnam**. Nixon's greatest success came in foreign policy. He introduced the one of the last major stages of the Cold War, **détente**. In Vietnam, he quickly began Vietnamization, reducing the number of U.S. troops. He based his actions on what was called the "Nixon Doctrine." The president said that the U.S. would no longer fight in Asia to stop communism. Instead, America would provide supplies and support, but leave the fighting to the nation's army. This was a major modification of the containment policy. Basically, the U.S. had been so hurt by Vietnam that it was no longer willing to fight for containment, only to pay for it. While he was scaling back, Nixon pushed hard for a peace agreement that would allow the Americans to leave entirely. Eventually, Congress also withdrew the Gulf of Tonkin Resolution and passed the War Powers Act that limited how long the president could send out troops without Congressional approval.

**Election of 1972**. The Democrats nominated Governor George McGovern of Alabama for president in 1972. Nixon easily took the Republican nomination. Vietnam was again a major issue. Nixon had reduced the number of U.S. ground troops, but was still using the president's authority to fight. McGovern called for an immediate withdrawal, regardless of the consequences. He also favored a number of liberal plans that pleased the radicals but not traditional Democrats. He hoped to get the full support of young people who could now vote since the 26th Amendment (1971) lowered the voting age from twenty-one to eighteen, but it did not happen. Right before the election Kissinger announced that "peace was at hand" in the negotiations with North Vietnam. Nixon won by a landslide with over 60% of the votes.

**Détente**. The break between the U.S.S.R. and China had been obvious for years, but it was Nixon who finally took advantage of it. He and his brilliant foreign policy advisor, later Secretary of State, Henry Kissinger, went back to traditional diplomacy. They treated the U.S.S.R. and China not as two parts of a massive communist alliance, but as rival nations. Nixon made peace overtures toward China, which had had no official contacts with the U.S. since 1949. Nixon's hope was that the Soviet Union would be threatened by a possible American-Chinese friendship. That threat might lead them to make their own offer of friendship with America to avoid being isolated. It was old "balance of power" diplomacy and it worked.

Nixon had made his reputation in politics as an anti-communist. So, when he announced that he would visit China in 1972, it was a national shock. Nixon also allowed China to join the United Nations and replace Taiwan on the Security Council. Taiwan was thrown completely out of the U.N. by the anti-American assembly and has never been allowed back. The China visit in 1972 produced goodwill, images of Nixon walking on the Great Wall and the beginning of direct talks between the two nations.

By the early 1970s, the Soviet Union was firmly under the control of Leonid Brezhnev. The threat of a U.S.-Chinese friendship, as well as the Soviet need for Western technology (the Free World was much better at developing new technology,) pushed Brezhnev to improve relations with the U.S. Nixon became the first U.S. president to visit the Soviet Union when

| President Nixon Visits China

he went in 1972 for a summit. The two sides signed SALT (Strategic Arms Limitation Treaty) and agreed not to increase their number of missiles for five years. They also signed agreements for cultural and technical cooperation.

Détente lasted through most of the 1970s, but the Soviet Union never truly wanted peace. It still worked in the Third World to create more communist nations. It used treaties and agreements to improve its weapons and power. It arrested its own citizens who argued for more freedom. Nixon had hoped that détente would open up the Iron Curtain nations to Western ideas and bring the fall of communism. It did not succeed at that time. Relations with China continued to improve even after détente ended in 1979, but that nation remained communist and a major rival power to the U.S. even after the end of the Cold War.

**Watergate**. Nixon's realistic approach to diplomacy and his moderate success at home would have left him with a fine legacy in history if not for Watergate. Watergate was the name of the scandal that eventually forced Richard Nixon to become the only U.S. president to resign from office. It began in June of 1972 when several men were caught trying to break into the Democratic National Party Headquarters in the Watergate building in Washington. They were carrying electronic equipment to "bug" the office and listen to what went on there. One of the men worked for the Committee for the Reelection of the President (CRP)! The burglars, a CRP employee, and a White House consultant were eventually convicted for the break-in. Nixon denied any knowledge of the burglary or of a cover-up among his aides to hide their involvement.

After the 1972 election, evidence was found linking several presidential aides to the burglary and a cover-up. An investigation began in May of 1973 when Nixon promised a full inquiry and appointed Archibald Cox as a special prosecutor. Cox and a Senate committee, led by Senator Sam Ervin, conducted a long, public investigation. One White House aide, John Dean, turned on the president, accusing him of covering up his aides' involvement in the burglary and using government agencies to harass his enemies, but there was no evidence to support Dean's story and Nixon denied it.

Then, it was discovered that Nixon had been secretly taping all conversations in his office since 1971. Cox and the committee asked for the tapes of Nixon's conversations with Dean to confirm or deny his version of what happened. Nixon refused, saying it would harm the authority of the president to reveal his private conversations. He offered to give Cox summaries of the tapes in October of 1973. When the prosecutor refused, Nixon ordered the Attorney General to fire him. The Attorney General and his assistant both resigned rather than fire Cox for doing his job. Their replacement finally

obeyed the president and fired Cox. This "Saturday night massacre" prompted the House to begin the impeachment process.

In October of 1973, Vice President Spiro Agnew resigned from office because of corruption charges unrelated to Watergate. Nixon appointed Representative Gerald Ford to replace Agnew under the procedure set up in the 25th Amendment. Ford was approved by the Senate and took office in December of 1973 as the nation's first appointed vice president.

Cox was replaced by Leon Jaworski who continued to press the investigation. When Nixon finally bowed to legal pressure and gave some of the tapes to a federal judge in late 1973, several key parts were missing or erased. In April of 1974, Jaworski obtained a **subpoena** for the needed tapes and related documents. In response, the president released over a thousand pages of written transcripts taken from the recordings. Still, Jaworski insisted on getting the tapes and the Supreme Court ruled in his favor in July of 1974. That same month, a House committee asked the whole body to vote on three articles of impeachment against the president for abuse of power and withholding evidence.

The end came in August. Under pressure, Nixon finally released the key missing transcripts which showed he had approved a cover-up just days after the burglary. At that point, Nixon lost all of his support in Congress. Impeachment was certain. He resigned on August 9, 1974 and Gerald Ford became president. Eventually, twenty-nine people went to jail for the burglary or related crimes of trying to hide White House involvement.

**Name the item, idea, or person.**

**2.48** Type of diplomacy used by Nixon and Kissinger with China and the U.S.S.R. _____

_____

**2.49** Cold War thaw of the 1970s _____

**2.50** The U.S. would use only money, not soldiers, to pursue containment in Asia _____

_____

**2.51** Soviet leader in the 1970s _____

**2.52** Favorite cause of the protesters of the 1960s and 70s _____

**2.53** People who clashed with police at the 1968 Democratic convention _____

_____

**2.54** The first U.S. president to visit the Soviet Union and Red (Communist) China _____

_____

**2.55** Scandal that ended Nixon's presidency _____

**2.56** Combination of a stagnate economy and inflation in the 1970s _____

_____

**2.57** First appointed vice president _____

**2.58** Place where National Guardsmen opened fire on protesters in May of 1970 _____

_____

**2.59** Sending children across town to school to achieve racial balance _____

_____

**2.60** Result of the 26th Amendment _____

**2.61** What the Watergate burglars were trying to do _____

_____

**2.62** Vice president who resigned in 1973 due to corruption charges _____

_____

**2.63** Names of the two special prosecutors for Watergate _____

_____

**2.64** China replaced this nation at the U.N. _____

**2.65** New Supreme Court Chief Justice, 1969 _____

**2.66** Law that limits how long the president can send out troops on his own authority _____

_____

**2.67** 1968 Democratic candidate _____

**2.68** 1972 Democratic candidate _____

**2.69** Two nuclear weapons agreements signed at 1972 U.S.-U.S.S.R. summit _____

_____

_____

**2.70** White House aide who first accused Nixon of a cover-up _____

_____

**2.71** Records kept by Nixon that were eventually used to prove his involvement in the cover-up

_____

**2.72** Leading anti-war candidate in 1968, assassinated _____

**2.73** Source of many of the social problems of the 1990s _____

_____

**2.74** Nixon's brilliant foreign policy advisor/Secretary of State _____

_____

**2.75** What did the youth of the 1960s reject? _____

_____

**Answer these questions.**

**2.76** Why was Nixon's visit to China such a shock? _____

_____

**2.77** What were two of the social results of the 1960s rebellion? _____

_____

_____

**2.78** How did Nixon deal with inflation? _____

_____

_____

**2.79** In your opinion, was Richard Nixon a good or bad president? Why? _____

_____

_____

_____

_____

_____

## TEACHER CHECK _____ _____

↺ **Review the material in this section in preparation for the Self Test.** This Self Test will check your mastery of this particular section as well as your knowledge of the previous section.

# SELF TEST 2

**Match the person with their description** (2 points, each answer).

2.01 _____ First appointed vice president

2.02 _____ North Vietnamese communist leader

2.03 _____ Youthful president, assassinated in 1963

2.04 _____ Civil rights leader, assassinated in 1968

2.05 _____ Anti-communist who was noted
for his false accusations

2.06 _____ First commander of NATO, president during
a time of prosperity and stability

2.07 _____ Commander in Korea, fired for insubordination

2.08 _____ President whose Great Society was strangled
by increased involvement in the Vietnam War

2.09 _____ Communist dictator of Cuba

2.010 _____ First president to visit Red China and the U.S.S.R and first to resign from office

a. Fidel Castro

b. Ho Chi Minh

c. Douglas MacArthur

d. Dwight D. Eisenhower

e. Richard M. Nixon

f. Gerald Ford

g. Martin Luther King

h. Lyndon B. Johnson

i. John F. Kennedy

j. Joseph McCarthy

**Name the item, person, or idea** (3 points, each answer).

2.011 America's primary Cold War policy, created by Harry Truman _____

_____

2.012 The incident that began the Civil Rights Movement _____

_____

_____

**2.013** Post-Civil War black educator who accepted segregation until blacks could build up their economic power _____

**2.014** Martin Luther King's speech at the Lincoln Memorial during the March on Washington

_____

**2.015** The biggest problem with the economy between 1945 and 1974

_____

**2.016** Kennedy's volunteer organization to aid the Third World

_____

**2.017** Barrier that divided East and West Berlin _____

**2.018** Cold War thaw of the 1970s _____

**2.019** President, approved the interstate highway system and the St. Lawrence Seaway _____

_____

_____

**2.020** Congressional resolution that gave the president a free hand in Vietnam

_____

_____

**2.021** First artificial satellite in space and the nation that launched it _____

_____

**2.022** Dwight D. Eisenhower's campaign slogan _____

**2.023** "Defensive alliance" of the Iron Curtain nations _____

**2.024** Kennedy's aid program for Latin America _____

**2.025** Harry S. Truman's legislative program _____

**Describe each of these incidents or item** (5 points, each answer).

**2.026** The Cuban Missile Crisis _____

_____

_____

_____

_____

**2.027** The Marshall Plan _____

_____

_____

_____

**2.028** The integration of Central High School in Little Rock, Arkansas, 1957 _____

_____

_____

_____

_____

**2.029** Watergate _____

_____

_____

_____

_____

**2.030** How the Civil Rights Movement challenged segregation _____

_____

_____

_____

_____

**2.031** The youth rebellion of the 1960s and early '70s _____

_____

_____

_____

_____

**2.032** The difference between *Plessy v. Ferguson* and *Brown v. Board of Education* _____

_____

_____

_____

| 80 / 100 | SCORE _____ | TEACHER _____ _____ |
| --- | --- | --- |
| | | initials           date |

# 3. UNEXPECTED VICTORY

Vietnam and Watergate shattered American self-confidence. Distrust of the government grew strong and deep. The nation began to doubt that communism could be defeated. America's European allies wanted peace with communism, not antagonism, even when the U.S.S.R. continued its attacks on freedom in the Third World and its own territory. However, an unexpected surprise lay ahead. The U.S.S.R. was about to be broken and the Iron Curtain torn down.

The last presidents of the Cold War had to deal with the aftershocks of Vietnam and Watergate in America. They also had to conduct the Cold War in the new reality that followed those traumatic events. That reality was a nation less willing to follow its leaders, less willing to fight, and suffering from reduced prestige abroad. Détente continued, but its success came under serious question until Soviet aggression ended it in 1979.

By the 1980s America began to heal and regain its composure as a nation. That decade finally saw communism collapse in Europe under the weight of its own stupidity. The world watched breathlessly as the Communist World fell apart and the Soviet Union followed. The Cold War ended with a victory for the Free World, the one side left standing when the dust cleared.

## SECTION OBJECTIVES

**Review these objectives**. When you have completed this section, you should be able to:

1. Describe the course of the Cold War and the incidents within it.
2. Name the presidents of the Cold War and the events that happened during their administration.
4. Describe events in America and changes in American thinking during the Cold War era.
5. Name the important people on both sides of the Cold War.

## VOCABULARY

**Study these words to enhance your learning success in this section**.

**fundamentalist** (fən də mənt l əst). A movement that stresses strict and literal adherence to a set of beliefs.

**infrastructure** (in' frə strək chər). The permanent installations required for military purposes, including: roads, bridges, airports, supply depots, etc.

## Aftershocks

**Gerald R. Ford (1913-2006)**. Gerald Ford was the only man to serve as both vice president and president without being elected to either office. He was born in Nebraska and raised in Grand Rapids, Michigan. He was strong and active in sports. He entered the University of Michigan in 1931 and was a valuable member of the school's football team. He graduated from Yale Law School in 1941 and joined the navy soon after the beginning of World War II. He served on the *U.S.S. Monterey*, which saw considerable action in the Pacific. He returned to his law career and became active in Republican politics after he was discharged. He ran for the U.S. House in 1948 and won. He was reelected to that office twelve times. In 1973 when Nixon chose him to replace vice president Spiro Agnew, Ford was the minority leader of the House (the highest ranking Republican).

**Pardon**. Ford was reasonably popular, honest, and easygoing. The nation was disgusted with Watergate and willing to give the new, appointed president a chance. However, one month after he took office, Ford issued a full pardon to Richard Nixon for any crimes he may have committed in office. The pardon severely damaged his popularity and added to the national distrust of the government.

**Home Problems**. As with Nixon, Ford's greatest problem was inflation. Ford launched an anti-inflation campaign in 1974 called "Whip Inflation Now" or WIN. For a time, the president wore a WIN button everywhere, as he worked to lower spending. The campaign triggered a recession and was quickly abandoned. Stagflation made the economy a difficult problem. Dealing with inflation caused unemployment, and dealing with unemployment caused inflation. It seemed to be a no-win situation.

Congress was controlled by the Democrats during the Ford Administration and little was accomplished. Former New York Governor Nelson Rockefeller (grandson of the Standard Oil Baron) was appointed vice president. Ford also set up an amnesty plan for the over 100,000 men who had avoided the draft or deserted during the Vietnam War. However, the program required the men to do public service work for two years; most refused. Congress also refused to grant Ford's request for more aid to South Vietnam in 1975 when the North launched the offensive that eventually conquered the South. The U.S. was not going to get involved in anything! "No more Vietnams" was a foreign policy law for many years.

**Mayaguez**. In May of 1975, a month after the fall of Vietnam, the Khmer Rouge in Cambodia seized a U.S. merchant ship, the *Mayaguez*, in international waters. Ford ordered a naval task force with Marine troops to attack. Thirty-eight men were killed, but the crew of the ship was rescued. Some people condemned the raid as too much, but the nation mainly supported Ford. They did not want petty dictators threatening Americans abroad.

**Election of 1976**. The nation celebrated its Bicentennial and an election in 1976. Ford narrowly won the Republican nomination after a tough primary fight with Governor Ronald Reagan of California. The Democrats nominated Jimmy Carter, Governor of Georgia, who had an excellent record on civil rights and an equally excellent history of honesty. Ford was handicapped by the poor opinion many people had of the government and the pardon, which tied him to the Watergate Scandal. Carter campaigned as an honest outsider who was not smeared by the taint of Washington muck. He won the election by a slim margin.

**James E. Carter (1924- )**. Commonly known as Jimmy, James Earl Carter was the first president to graduate from the U.S. Naval Academy. He was born and raised in Plains, Georgia. His father owned a farm and store in town. He attended public schools and graduated from the Naval Academy in 1946. He served in the navy until 1953, working on the development of the first nuclear powered submarines. In 1953 his father died, and Jimmy left the navy to run the family peanut business. He was an astute manager and the business prospered.

Carter became active in community projects and politics, serving on the local Board of Education, among others. He also opposed segregation, and was one of only a few to vote against banning blacks in his church. He ran for the state senate in 1962. He won the Democratic nomination only after he successfully charged that his opponent won by violating the voting laws. He then won the election. He was reelected in 1964, but was defeated in the primary when he ran for governor in 1966. He tried again in 1970 and won. He was unknown outside of Georgia when he decided to run for president in 1976. He built his reputation by campaigning hard and winning early primary elections. He won the nomination against 10 opponents.

Jimmy Carter won the 1976 election as a Washington outsider and that was his undoing. He did not know how to work with the U.S. Congress and had no experience in foreign policy. It showed as he frequently changed positions and failed to establish any clear, achievable goals. His administration quickly began to look confused and naive as it faced stagflation, an energy crisis, the end of détente and a major hostage crisis.

**Energy Problems**. The nation of Israel had been created by the U.N. in 1948, displacing the Arabs of Palestine. The Arab nations around Israel never accepted it. Israel and its Arab neighbors fought wars in 1948, 1956, and 1967. In October of 1973, a fourth war began when Egypt and Syria attacked Israel on Yom Kippur, the holiest Jewish holiday. As with all the previous wars, Israel won the Yom Kippur War. It was ended by a cease fire due to U.N. and American mediation.

Several of the Arab nations were members of OPEC (Organization of Petroleum Exporting Countries). In 1973 OPEC put an embargo on oil sales to all nations that supported Israel, including the U.S. The embargo held for five months and drove oil prices up dramatically. OPEC used its control over the supply of oil to drive up prices through the 1970s. Oil shortages led to lines at the gas pumps again in 1973 and 1979 as gas stations rationed gas to conserve their supply.

Jimmy Carter pushed hard from the beginning of his administration for the creation of an intelligent energy policy. American's love of the automobile and cheap gas made energy

| The Camp David Accords

controls unpopular. However, a national energy program was passed in 1978 that included a new Department of Energy. The laws taxed cars with poor gas mileage, required businesses to cut petroleum use, and forced higher prices to encourage conservation. These measures drove up the price of oil and added to inflation, hurting Carter's popularity. By the 1980s expanding oil production drove the prices down and ended the "energy crisis" for the time being.

The president appointed Paul Volcker to the Federal Reserve Board in 1979. He began a new policy at the board aimed at controlling inflation by control of the money supply. Using the "Fed's" power to charge interest on money loaned to banks, he forced up the interest rates. The high interest rates caused another recession, but they also tamed inflation which began to slow in the 1980s.

**Foreign Policy Successes**. Carter had a few successes in foreign policy. His greatest was mediating an agreement between Egypt and Israel. The Egyptian president, Anwar Sadat, had risked his position in the Arab world by visiting Israel and opening negotiations to end the long hostility between the two nations. When negotiations stalled, Jimmy Carter invited the leaders of both nations to America for direct talks. The result was an agreement called the Camp David Accords. Under it, Egypt recognized Israel and Israel returned the Sinai Peninsula, which it had taken in the last war. Sadat and Menachem Begin, Prime Minister of Israel, won the Nobel Peace Prize for their efforts.

Jimmy Carter also completed long standing negotiations with Panama over the fate of the Panama Canal. The two treaties arranged for the canal to be gradually turned over to Panamanian control by the year 2000 and for it to be neutral, open to all shipping. Both treaties were ratified in the Senate by close votes in 1978. The U.S. kept the right to use armed force to protect the canal.

Carter continued the Nixon policy toward China. In 1979 the U.S. and China established formal diplomatic relations and exchanged ambassadors. He developed better relations with the nations of Africa, but he also seemed helpless as the Soviets expanded their influence there.

**Death of Détente**. Jimmy Carter the idealist, made human rights the centerpiece of his foreign policy. However, it was difficult to press for human rights among sensitive allies like the Philippines and South Korea. The Soviet Union resented Carter's push for them to grant their own people more freedom. They quickly and publicly refused Carter's suggestions for deep cuts in nuclear weapons. Finally, Carter got the SALT talks back on track and got a new treaty limiting weapons expansion. Critics said it favored the Soviets, and SALT II stalled in Congress.

Struggling détente died a sudden death in December of 1979, when the Soviet Union invaded Afghanistan to protect a pro-Soviet government on their southern border. They installed a puppet ruler and quickly became bogged down in a brutal guerrilla war. The Soviets were able to hold the cities, but they could never take the mountainous countryside

| Ayatollah Khomeini

defended by Muslim rebels using U.S. and Chinese weapons. Afghanistan has been called the Soviet Vietnam.

Carter had to react to this blatant aggression. He halted sales of grain and technology to the U.S.S.R. He withdrew SALT II from consideration by the Senate (although both sides honored the limits set in the treaty). He withdrew the U.S. from the 1980 Olympics in Moscow (only a few other nations did so). He also restarted draft registration (cancelled after Vietnam) and increased military spending. Détente was finished and the Cold War continued.

**Iran Hostage Crisis**. Carter's presidency is remembered most for the crisis in Iran. Shah Mohammad Reza Pahlavi was the ruler of Iran in the 1970s. He was a faithful U.S. ally, but also a ruthless dictator. His attempts to modernize Iran were deeply resented by his conservative Muslim people. With his emphasis on human rights, Carter did not offer the Shah much support as his people began to rebel. In 1979 a Muslim religious leader named Ayatollah

Khomeini overthrew the Shah and set up a **fundamentalist** Muslim government very hostile to America.

Later that same year, Carter allowed the exiled Shah to come to the U.S. for medical treatment. Demonstrators outside the U.S. Embassy in Iran attacked the compound in November and took the staff hostage with the tacit support of the government. This was an unbelievable violation of centuries of international law that required nations to protect the embassy staff of foreign countries! The militants holding the hostages demanded the return of the Shah for trial. Carter refused, froze Iranian assets in the U.S. and broke diplomatic relations. After months of fruitless negotiations, Carter authorized a military rescue which ended in a disaster, crashing in the desert without engaging the enemy.

The crisis and the botched rescue damaged U.S. prestige abroad. Americans could not believe that 52 American embassy staff people could be treated this way without any successful U.S. response. Carter's prestige at home fell. Finally, Iran and Iraq got into a destructive war (1980-88) that forced Iran to seek the return of its frozen American assets. The hostages were released after 444 days in captivity, but in a final insult, not until just hours after Carter left office in 1981. They came back to a tumultuous welcome in the U.S. Washington was covered in yellow ribbons, which had become a symbol that the nation was waiting and praying for their safe return.

**Election of 1980**. By the time of the elections in 1980, Carter's popularity had plummeted very low. He was challenged for the Democratic nomination by Senator Edward Kennedy, another brother of the late president. It was a close contest, but Carter eventually won the nomination due to moral problems in Kennedy's life. The Republicans nominated Governor Ronald Reagan, who chose George Bush for his running mate. Reagan's good looks, poise, and positive outlook for America caught the attention of the voters. He won the election by a substantial majority, leaving Carter to depart, beaten, and bedraggled.

Jimmy Carter, however, was not a man to retire to a rocking chair. He made good use of his prestige as a former president in a number of ways. He became a leading spokesman and worker for Habitat for Humanity, an organization that builds homes for the working poor. He has led numerous efforts to negotiate peace and monitor free elections. He was, for example, instrumental in convincing Haiti's military government to step down before a U.S. invasion in 1994. He has fulfilled the high calling of a statesman with dignity and integrity since leaving the White House.

 **Complete these sentences.**

**3.1** Jimmy Carter emphasized _____ in his foreign policy.

**3.2** Détente was ended by the Soviet _____ in 1979.

**3.3** Control of the oil supply by _____ caused an energy crisis in the 1970s.

**3.4** Ford tried to end inflation with his _____ campaign.

**3.5**  Carter's presidency is remembered most for the _____

_____ .

**3.6**  The Federal Reserve Board finally brought inflation under control in the 1980s

by controlling the _____ .

**3.7**  Carter won the 1976 election by running as an _____

_____ .

**3.8**  Ford ordered a navy task force to rescue the crew of the _____

in 1975.

**3.9**  The most controversial action of Ford's administration was when he _____

_____ .

**3.10**  Jimmy Carter got the Senate to ratify two treaties that gave the _____

to _____ by the year 2000.

**3.11**  The U.S. established formal relations with _____ in 1979.

**3.12**  Jimmy Carter mediated between Sadat and Begin to reach the _____

that paved the way for peace between Egypt and Israel.

**3.13**  Ford's appointed vice president was _____ .

**3.14**  Jimmy Carter reacted to the invasion of Afghanistan by _____ the

Olympics in Moscow and _____ SALT II.

**3.15**  Radicals in Iran held _____ American embassy personnel hostage for

_____ days (1979-81).

**3.16**  _____ was the Muslim religious leader who over-

threw Shah _____ in Iran.

**3.17**  Iran finally negotiated the release of the hostages when it needed money for its war with

_____ .

**3.18**  Jimmy Carter defeated _____ to get the 1980 Demo-

cratic nomination.

**3.19**  _____ was elected president in 1980.

## Healing and Change

**Ronald W. Reagan (1911-2004).** Ronald Wilson Reagan was the oldest man ever elected president (69). He was born and raised in Illinois. His father was a shoe salesman. Ronald, nicknamed "Dutch," attended public schools and worked his way through Eureka College, graduating in 1932. He started working as a radio announcer for the Chicago Cubs in Illinois.

He made a screen test for Warner Brothers Studio in 1937, and was hired as an actor. He appeared in over fifty movies between 1937 and 1964. He joined the Air Force during World War II, but poor eyesight forced him to make training films for most of the war. He was elected president of the Screen Actors Guild (the actors union) in 1947, and served in that post for many years.

Reagan became more conservative over time. He cooperated with efforts to remove suspected communists from the movie industry in the 1950s. He joined the Republican Party in 1960. He was elected governor of California in 1966 and reelected in 1970. He was defeated by Gerald Ford for the 1976 Republican presidential nomination, but won it in 1980. He was elected president that year by a large majority.

**Terrorism.** In the 1980s, unrest in the Middle East caused a wave of terrorism. The U.S. was mainly affected by Arab terrorists who objected to American support for the nation of Israel. The Palestine Liberation Organization (PLO) and radical groups supported by Iran or Libya were among the most active.

Several terrorist attacks killed or endangered Americans during the decade. In 1983 U.S. marines were in Lebanon trying to support a cease fire in a bitter war there. A suicide bomber drove a truck filled with explosives into their barracks. More than 200 men died. In 1985 a TWA jet was seized by terrorists after leaving Italy. One American was killed, but the rest of the passengers were eventually released. Later that same year an Italian cruise ship, the *Achille Lauro,* was hijacked and again one American was killed.

In 1986 terrorists planted a bomb in a German disco used by U.S. soldiers. President Reagan ordered the bombing of terrorist camps in Libya when the evidence connected them to the bombing. That strong reaction caused a decline in Libyan-sponsored terrorism.

Beirut, Lebanon was a center of terrorist activity because a brutal civil war had left it without any effective government. In the 1980s, dozens of American, European, and Israeli citizens were captured and held hostage in the city, some for years. Some died in captivity or were killed. The U.S. had no way to locate or negotiate with those holding the hostages, and it was a frustrating experience.

**Reaganomics.** Ronald Reagan wanted to reduce the size and influence of the federal government. Reporters called his program *Reaganomics*. He reduced taxes, cut welfare programs, and worked to reduce the power of federal agencies that regulated businesses. Reagan was also a firm believer in a strong military to protect America against communism. He increased military spending significantly. The increased spending and lower taxes caused huge budget deficits. The national debt under Reagan grew from $907.7 billion in 1980 to $2,602.3 billion in 1988.

The economy had gone into a recession after high interest rates were set up to tame inflation in the late 1970s, but by the end of Reagan's first term the recession had ended and a long recovery began. More importantly, inflation did not rise again. Prices rose only slowly as the nation began to prosper again.

**Home Notes.** Reagan faced a wide variety of problems and events at home in his first term. He was shot in the chest during an assassination attempt in March of 1981. He survived and recovered quickly. He fired many of the nation's air traffic controllers that same year when they disobeyed an order to end a strike. He appointed the first woman to the U.S. Supreme Court, Sandra Day O'Connor. In 1984 the new Space Shuttle Program (begun in 1981) was temporarily halted by an accident. In 1986 the shuttle *Challenger* blew up after takeoff, killing all aboard including a special guest, a school teacher.

**Foreign Affairs**. Reagan took a very hard line in dealing with the Soviet Union. He was deeply opposed to communism and the expansion of the Soviet "evil empire." He had tremendous faith in the American people and their system of government. His self-confidence was contagious and it made him very popular. He did a great deal to restore American self-confidence after the traumas of the 1970s.

Many Americans also realized that the years of détente had not ended or even slowed Soviet aggression. Reagan, therefore, had public support as he built up military power, invested in more advanced missile technology, challenged Soviet power whenever he could, and tried to revive containment. Vietnam was still enough of an issue that Reagan did not have a free hand to contain communism. However, he often gave support to groups fighting pro-Soviet governments. Two of Reagan's main efforts were in Central America and the Caribbean.

Prior to 1979, the nation of Nicaragua was ruled by a family of dictators named the Somoza. They were overthrown that year by the Sandinista, a communist-style guerrilla group. They set up an oppressive government that received most of its support from Cuba and the Soviet Union. The Sandinistas were also funneling Soviet weapons to rebel groups in nearby Honduras and El Salvador.

Reagan sent U.S. aid to both Honduras and El Salvador. He also sent aid to the *Contras*, a group that was created to fight a guerrilla war against the Sandinista government in Nicaragua. However, evidence of massacres and cruelty by both sides caused many Americans

| Ronald Reagan

to question getting involved. Congress eventually cut off all money for aid to the *Contras* due both to the fear of getting too involved (Vietnam disease) and distaste for the brutal actions of the *Contras*.

The small island nation of Grenada in the Caribbean had also come under the control of a pro-Soviet, communist-style government in 1979. The new regime began to build a massive airstrip that the U.S. feared would be used as a Soviet air base. In October of 1983, a revolution broke out and a communist leader was killed. Many of the other Caribbean nations were very nervous about having a communist government so near. They asked the U.S. to help. Concerned for the many Americans on the island, Reagan agreed. In October of 1983, American and Caribbean soldiers invaded the island, threw out the Cuban "advisors" and set up a democratic government. The action was very popular in the U.S., but was condemned elsewhere.

In 1983 the president proposed a controversial new program to develop a missile defense system for the U.S. that would be set up in orbit above the earth. Called the Strategic Defense Initiative, it was labeled "Star Wars" by its opponents. Many people questioned investing a huge amount of money to expand the Cold War into space. The peace groups opposed it. However, Congress approved some money for the program because there was evidence the U.S.S.R. was already working on its own Star Wars program.

**Election of 1984**. The economy was in good shape in 1984, and inflation was finally under control. Reagan was very popular and was easily renominated. In fact, many of his opponents called him the "teflon president" because nothing they accused him of stuck! He was opposed by Walter Mondale, who had been Jimmy Carter's vice president. Mondale's running mate was Geraldine Ferraro, a member of the U.S. House and the first woman to run on a major party ticket. Reagan won the election by the largest majority in U.S. history. He was victorious in 49 states and took all but 13 electoral votes.

**Changes in the U.S.S.R.** In the 1980s changes began in the Soviet Union that would finally bring the Cold War to a close. The cautious, fearful leaders who had survived under Stalin finally began to die. Brezhnev died in 1982. The next Soviet leader, Yuri Andropov died in 1984. His successor, Konstantin Chernenko died in 1985. At his death, a much younger man, Mikhail Gorbachev, came to power and began astonishing changes.

Gorbachev was one of a group of new party leaders who realized the Soviet Union was in serious trouble. The cost of paying for revolutions all over the world was too much for the U.S.S.R. to continue. Its own economy was in very weak shape. Under communism, people cannot be fired from their jobs and don't receive more pay for better work. Thus, most people just do the least they can. Soviet industries were badly out of date because no one had any reason to build new or better

| George H. W. Bush

equipment. Soviet citizens could not get the goods they wanted and needed. The U.S.S.R. was not developing the new computer technology that was so rapidly changing life in the Free World. In short, Gorbachev and his supporters recognized that things needed to change, immediately!

Gorbachev tried to rearrange the Soviet economy to be more productive. He began a series of reforms called *perestroika* (restructuring). He encouraged more freedom of speech called *glasnost* (openness) to allow new ideas to push changes in the economy. He also tried to improve relations with the Free World to get money, technology, and to reduce the costs of the Cold War. However, his reforms did not change the state control of production and failed to stop the collapse of the Soviet economy. In fact, the new openness would eventually destroy communist control.

**American Reaction**. Gorbachev quickly became very popular in the West, especially in Western Europe. Reagan, however, did not trust the changes he was seeing in the U.S.S.R.

The Soviets had lied too many times in the past about what they were doing. Also, the communist party could easily have decided the reforms were too much and stop them at any time. Many people condemned Reagan for his caution.

The president did agree to meet several times with Gorbachev. He asked the new leader to match his words with deeds. In 1987 Gorbachev began to do so by signing the Intermediate-Range Nuclear Forces Treaty. This treaty committed both sides to <u>destroy</u> an entire group of weapons. It was the first treaty to actually <u>reduce</u>, not limit, the number of nuclear weapons.

**Iran-Contra Affair**. Reagan was very disturbed by the continued holding of American hostages in Beirut. The terrorists there were supported by Iran which had terrible relations with the U.S. since the taking of the American embassy in 1979. Reagan decided to sell weapons to Iran (which needed them for the war with Iraq) in the hopes of winning freedom for the hostages. This was done in secret because American policy forbade dealing with terrorists. Iran took the weapons, but only three hostages were freed.

Reagan's aides used the profits from the weapon sales to help the *Contras*. This was illegal because Congress had forbidden any U.S. funds to be used for the *Contras*. The activity was exposed in 1987. A Congressional investigation found that several White House aides had acted illegally and blamed Reagan for not controlling his staff better.

Several of Reagan's aides were convicted, but the convictions were overturned on appeal or the men were pardoned by President Bush in 1992. The only thing proven against Reagan was poor management. He left office in 1989, still very popular. In 1994 he announced he had Alzheimer's disease which slowly robbed him of his ability to think and remember. After that, he lived the rest of his life, out of the public eye, under his wife's care.

**Election of 1988**. George H. W. Bush won the Republican nomination in 1988. He chose Senator Dan Quayle of Indiana as his running mate. The Democrats picked Michael Dukakis (Governor of Mass.), who ran with Senator Lloyd Bentsen of Texas. The Democrats tried to push the Iran-Contra Affair in the election and attacked Reagan's cut backs in welfare services. Bush attacked Dukakis for his lack of experience in foreign policy and accused him of being too easy on criminals. The strong economy, Reagan's popularity and Bush's long experience gave him the presidency by a comfortable margin.

 **Complete these items.**

**3.20** Why did Reagan sell arms to Iran? _____

_____

_____

**3.21** Describe the secret activity of the Iran-Contra Affair. _____

_____

_____

_____

_____

**3.22** List four acts of terrorism in the 1980s.

a. _____

b. _____

c. _____

d. _____

**3.23** Give the Russian name and a description of Gorbachev's two major reforms.

a. _____

b. _____

**3.24** Why did Reagan oppose the Sandinista government? _____

_____

_____

**3.25** Name four parts of Reaganomics.

a. _____

b. _____

c. _____

d. _____

**3.26** Describe what happened on Grenada in October, 1983. _____

_____

_____

_____

**3.27** What was so important about the Intermediate-Range Nuclear Forces Treaty? _____

_____

_____

**3.28** How many leaders did the Soviet Union have from 1981 to 1986? _____

**3.29** List three reasons why the Soviet economy was in trouble in the 1980s.

a. _____

b. _____

c. _____

**3.30** What American economic problem of the 1960s and 70s was controlled in the 1980s? _____

_____

**3.31** Name the first woman appointed to the Supreme Court. _____

_____

**3.32** What was "Star Wars?" (Give the real name and a description) _____

_____

_____

**3.33** What group was fired by Reagan for continuing a strike? _____

_____

## Miraculous Victory

**George H. W. Bush (1924- )**. George Herbert Walker Bush made his fortune in the oil business before entering government service. He was born to a successful businessman in Massachusetts. His family lived in Connecticut during his childhood, spending their summers in Maine. George attended private schools and entered the navy when he graduated in 1942. He became the navy's youngest pilot in 1943. In 1944 he was shot down during an attack on a Japanese held island. He succeeded in damaging his target before he jumped safely into the ocean. He was rescued by a submarine and received the Distinguished Flying Cross for his valor.

After the war, he entered Yale University, graduating in 1948. Instead of going into business with his father, George moved to Texas and got into the oil business. He worked his way up and earned a fortune on the way. He became interested in politics in the 1950s, working in the local Republican Party. He served in the U.S. House from 1967-1970. He was defeated in a run for the Senate in 1970. He served several appointed positions after that including Ambassador to the U.N., Chairman of the Republican National Committee, U.S. representative to China and Director of the Central Intelligence Agency. He tried for the 1980 Republican nomination for president, but lost to Ronald Reagan, who chose him as a running mate. As Reagan's vice president, Bush was an active member of the president's team. He was kept well informed of the president's decisions and was one of his advisors. He easily won the presidency in 1988.

**Savings and Loan Crisis**. The biggest domestic problem under Bush was the Savings and Loan Crisis. Lax rules, fraud, and bad debts caused over a thousand Savings and Loans (which are basically banks) to close in the 1980s. Many others were close to bankruptcy. The money people deposited in the S&Ls was insured by the federal government. So, the government had to cover these losses.

President Bush signed legislation in 1989 to deal with the crisis. The shaky S&Ls were taken by the government, depositors were paid, fraud was prosecuted, and the businesses that still had some value were sold to new investors. The total cost to the American taxpayers was estimated to be hundreds of billions of dollars. The legislation also tightened controls to prevent another financial disaster like this one.

**Miracle Year**. To any person who lived during the Cold War, 1989 was a year of miracles. In 1988 and 1989 the Soviet Union withdrew its troops from Afghanistan. It also reduced the number of soldiers and weapons it kept in the Iron Curtain nations of Europe. Most important of all, Gorbachev made it clear that the Soviet Union would not use force to maintain the communist governments of Eastern Europe! Anyone who believed those communist governments were supported by their people quickly learned otherwise. In the space of one short year, massive street demonstrations behind the Iron Curtain forced communism to disintegrate in Europe.

The speed and scope of the collapse was breathtaking. Hungary made sweeping changes to its constitution in 1989 that allowed non-communist parties to nominate candidates. A reform party won the first free elections that year. Poland had allowed an anti-communist union, Solidarity, for a time in the 1980s. However, the threat of a Soviet invasion led to martial law and the banning of Solidarity. In 1989 it was again allowed and the government held partly free elections. Solidarity candidates won most of the offices. The communist party was dissolved in 1990 and completely free elections were held the next year.

In Czechoslovakia, thousands of people took to the streets demanding reforms. The communist party gave up its hold on power and Václav Havel, an anti-communist playwright became president. Free elections were held in 1990. The change was so smooth that it was called the Velvet Revolution. (The nation divided in 1992 to form the Czech Republic and Slovakia).

Demonstrations in Bulgaria forced the resignation and arrest of the communist leader. Greater freedom was given to the people in 1989 and free elections were held in 1990. In Romania an armed revolt captured and executed the barbaric dictator, Ceausescu, ending communist rule in that nation in 1989. It held free elections the following year.

The most vivid images of change were in Germany which had been divided since World War II, a living symbol of the Cold War. East German citizens not only demonstrated in 1989, they also left. Hungary had opened its borders earlier in the year. So, thousands of East Germans went through Hungary to Austria and then up to West Germany where they were automatically given citizenship.

| Crowds Gather as the Berlin Wall Comes Down

Pressured by demonstrations and the drain on its population, East Germany announced on November 9, 1989 that it was opening its borders with West Germany, including the Berlin Wall. Within hours people were climbing over the wall to join a huge street party on both sides of Berlin. Then, they took sledge hammers and began to tear down the Wall of Shame, the most notorious symbol of the Iron Curtain. The joyful, willful destruction of the Berlin Wall was the most vivid and enduring memory of the Miracle Year. East Germany held free elections and reunited with West Germany in 1990.

**Panama**. The situation in Panama had become very tense in the 1980s. The government there came under the control of General Manuel Noriega early in the decade. Noriega engaged in election fraud, corruption, and drug trafficking. He was indicted in the U.S. on charges of smuggling drugs into America. The president of Panama dismissed Noriega from his military position, but Noriega forced the president out of office. New elections in 1989 were won by

Guillermo Endara, a political enemy of Noriega. The general invalidated the election. In the unrest that followed, a U.S. soldier in the Canal Zone was killed.

Based on the charges against Noriega, the invalidation of a free election and the threat to U.S. soldiers in the Canal Zone, President Bush ordered the invasion of Panama in December. It was quickly successful and a new civilian government was set up. Noriega surrendered. He was found guilty of drug trafficking and sentenced to 40 years in prison in the U.S.

**Domestic Problems**. Bush faced a variety of problems at home. He had promised not to raise taxes, but did so in 1990 to cut the deficit. That decision hurt his popularity and was used against him in the 1992 campaign. High rates of crime, drug abuse, and social problems were blamed on the president who could not do much with the still Democratic Congress. In 1989 the oil tanker *Exxon Valdez* hit a reef near Alaska, causing the worst oil spill in U.S. history. The eleven million gallon spill was cleaned up by the military and federal government after the company did not do enough. In 1992 major riots in Los Angeles spread to other cities after white police officers were acquitted of beating a black man, Rodney King, even though the beating had been videotaped. Federal troops were sent in to establish order and Bush released federal funds to help with the clean up afterward.

**Persian Gulf War**. The Persian Gulf War was George H. W. Bush's greatest success. It also restored the nation's faith in the military that had been so badly damaged in Vietnam. It began in August of 1990 when the dictator of Iraq, Saddam Hussein, invaded the neighboring nation of Kuwait. Hussein was a brutal ruler who had built the fifth largest army in the world with Soviet Cold War support. He conquered Kuwait, a moderate nation with ties to the U.S., to gain control of its oil wealth. He expected the U.S. would not be able to stop him. He was very, very wrong.

George H. W. Bush, who had a long history of diplomatic training, quickly put together a coalition of almost 40 nations under the banner of the United Nations. Led by the U.S., these nations sent troops, tanks, aircraft, bombs, and supplies to neighboring Saudi Arabia to protect it from a possible Iraqi attack and prepare for an invasion of Kuwait. The U.N. gave Hussein until January 15, 1991 to leave Kuwait or the coalition would "use all necessary means" to force him out.

The coalition forces were under the command of American General Norman Schwarzkopf. "Stormin Norman" and his superior, General Colin Powell, Chairman of the Joint Chiefs of Staff, were the first generals to become national heroes since World War II. Also nicknamed "the Bear," Schwarzkopf was a tall, imposing man who dominated the televised press briefings that introduced him to the world. He commanded both "Operation Desert Shield," the protection of Saudi Arabia, and "Operation Desert Storm," the invasion and liberation of Kuwait.

When Hussein failed to meet the January 15 deadline, Operation Desert Storm began on January 16th with the largest air war in history. Using advanced Western technology, "smart bombs" with guidance systems destroyed Iraqi communication, transportation, radar, military, and airport facilities. Then, coalition aircraft began a massive bombing campaign directed against the Iraqi **infrastructure** and the soldiers dug in along the border of Kuwait. The Iraqi air force was quickly eliminated as an effective fighting force. Many of the surviving planes and pilots fled to Iran.

Iraq tried to get Israel into the war by firing "Scud" missiles at Israeli cities, which did limited damage and killed some people. Hussein hoped that if Israel attacked Iraq, the Arab members of the coalition would pull out rather than fight with their most hated enemy. Israel stayed out of the war in spite of the attacks.

Their willingness to let the coalition handle Hussein won international respect.

The intense five week long air war destroyed much of the Iraqi war machine and decimated army morale. Soldiers at the front began to desert in large numbers. As much as half the Iraqi army may have left before the land battle started. Once it did begin, thousands of Iraqi soldiers surrendered without firing a single shot.

The Iraqi commanders were expecting a direct assault on their defenses along the Kuwait border. Also, the U.S. Marines had been very publicly practicing amphibious assaults. So, the defenders prepared extensively for an assault from the Persian Gulf. In fact, no amphibious assault was planned. With all of Hussein's radar and air power destroyed, he was blind. He could only guess where the land assault would come, but with his typical arrogance Hussein promised it would be the "mother of all battles."

Knowing Hussein could not see where the coalition forces were, Schwarzkopf shifted a large portion of his army north, beyond the edge of the Iraqi defenses. On February 24th, the land war began. Coalition forces swept into Iraq behind the Iraqi forces in Kuwait. The army assaulting Kuwait made rapid progress as the Iraqi soldiers surrendered en masse. Hussein ordered a retreat after two days, but it was too late. The army was trapped.

The land war lasted only 100 hours, and destroyed most of the Iraqi army. George H. W. Bush ordered the attack halted after Kuwait was liberated and it was clear that further assaults would just be a massacre. One of the most gruesome sights of the war was the highway from Kuwait City to Iraq. Iraqi soldiers had looted the city, stealing anything they could to take with them as they ran for home. The road was covered with the remains of thousands of vehicles and men, destroyed by allied bombing, caught in the act of mass theft.

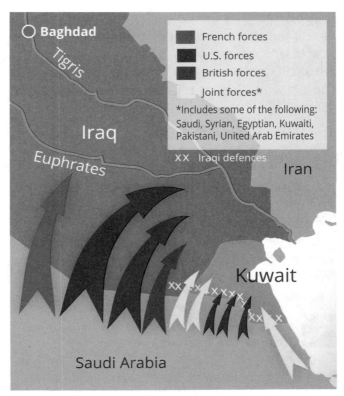

| Operation Desert Storm

**Effects of the War**. A large rebellion broke out against Saddam Hussein in Iraq after the war, but he was able to quell it. He had ordered his men to set the oil wells of Kuwait on fire as they fled. At the war's end, the air in Kuwait was black from the smoke of over 600 oil fires, the sun invisible. With tremendous innovation and effort the fires were all extinguished within nine months.

America lost only about 150 men in the war and U.S. prestige soared to new heights. The new atmosphere in the Middle East prompted the PLO to open negotiations with Israel to create a homeland for the Palestinian Arabs. Moreover, shortly after the war, the Western hostages held in Lebanon were released.

**Cold War Finale**. A war like this would not have been possible even a few years earlier. Cold War fears would have stopped it. However, the Soviet Union, needing to keep its goodwill with the West, quietly supported the war.

It appeared as if the Cold War was finally finished, but there was still one danger. Within the Soviet Union were older communist leaders, who still held power and might try to restore the old way. They made their move in August, 1991.

The Union of Soviet Socialist Republics was made up of fifteen "republics" that supposedly were part of the "union." (Many had "joined" the union by force.) In 1989 the U.S.S.R. had its first contested elections. Only communist party members could run, but those that favored reform were elected in large numbers. Boris Yeltsin was elected as president of the largest "republic," Russia.

The new reformers began to demand more self-government for the republics. In August of 1991, Gorbachev was to sign an agreement giving the republics more independence. That was the last straw for the old style communist leadership. They arrested Gorbachev and called in the military to restore the old order. Boris Yeltsin led a dedicated opposition, and within a few days the coup collapsed. Power fell into the hands of the presidents of the republics. They dissolved the U.S.S.R. by the end of the year, creating fifteen new nations. With the enemy gone, the victorious United States was at last miraculously free of the Soviet threat. The Cold War was finally over.

**Choose the correct nation.**

3.34 _____ Václav Havel, Velvet Revolution

3.35 _____ Destruction of the Berlin Wall
after the borders were opened

3.36 _____ Solidarity temporarily stopped
by martial law

3.37 _____ Changed its constitution and
held free elections in 1989

3.38 _____ Invaded by the U.S. in 1989

3.39 _____ Armed revolt killed Ceausescu

3.40 _____ Conquered by Iraq in 1990

3.41 _____ Yeltsin led the successful defense of the
reforms against the old communist leaders

a. Soviet Union

b. Hungary

c. Germany

d. Romania

e. Czechoslovakia

f. Poland

g. Kuwait

h. Panama

**Name the item, person, nation, or event.**

**3.42** Largest domestic crisis of the George H. W. Bush Administration

_____

**3.43** Oil tanker that caused the worst oil spill in U.S. history

_____

**3.44** Reason for the riots in 1992 in Los Angeles

_____

_____

**3.45** Year in which communism collapsed in Europe _____

**3.46** Year the Soviet Union was dissolved _____

**3.47** War to drive Iraqi army out of Kuwait _____

**3.48** U.S. commander of Desert Shield and Desert Storm

_____

**3.49** Panamanian strongman, put in U.S. jail for drug trafficking

_____

**3.50** Head of the Joint Chiefs of Staff during Desert Shield and Desert Storm

_____

**3.51** Dictator of Iraq _____

**Answer these questions.**

**3.52** What was the coalition strategy for the land attack on Kuwait? _____

_____

_____

**3.53** Why were there so many reformers in office in the U.S.S.R. in 1991? _____

_____

**3.54** Why was the Iraqi army blind by the time the land war began in Desert Storm? _____

_____

**3.55** How many new nations were created out of the old Soviet Union? _____

_____

**Before you take this last Self Test, you may want to do one or more of these self checks.**

1. _____ Read the objectives. See if you can do them.
2. _____ Restudy the material related to any objectives that you cannot do.
3. _____ Use the **SQ3R** study procedure to review the material:
   a. **S**can the sections.
   b. **Q**uestion yourself.
   c. **R**ead to answer your questions.
   d. **R**ecite the answers to yourself.
   e. **R**eview areas you did not understand.
4. _____ Review all vocabulary, activities, and Self Tests, writing a correct answer for every wrong answer.

# SELF TEST 3

**Name the item, event, or crisis** (each numbered answer, 3 points).

**3.01** Scandal that forced Richard Nixon to resign _____

_____

**3.02** Biggest economic problem of the 1960s and 70s _____

_____

**3.03** Crisis that marked Jimmy Carter's presidency, began when the deposed Shah of _____

Iran came to the U.S. for medical treatment, lasted 444 days _____

_____

**3.04** City in the Middle East where Americans were held hostage until after Operation _____

Desert Storm _____

**3.05** Reagan scandal over arms sales with the profits being used to fund a revolt against the

pro-Soviet Sandinistas in Nicaragua _____

_____

**3.06** Miraculous event in the Cold War in 1989 _____

_____

**3.07** War to drive Iraqi army out of Kuwait, 1990-91 _____

_____

**3.08** Action taken by Gerald Ford that made him very unpopular and tied him to the Nixon

scandal _____

**3.09** Action by the U.S.S.R. that ended détente in 1979 _____

_____

**3.010** Agreement made in the U.S. with the help of Jimmy Carter that allowed for peace between

Egypt and Israel _____

_____

**3.011** Incident that began the modern Civil Rights movement in 1955 _____

_____

_____

**3.012** Crisis under John Kennedy over nuclear weapons in Cuba _____

_____

**3.013** U.S. sponsored plan to rebuild Europe after World War II to prevent communism _____

_____

**3.014** Name the three Blocs of the Cold War era _____

_____

_____

_____

**3.015** The main Cold War policy of the U.S. toward communism, Truman created it _____

_____

**Match the person with the description** (each answer, 2 points).

| | | | |
|---|---|---|---|
| **3.016** | _____ | Dictator of Iraq | a. Jimmy Carter |
| **3.017** | _____ | Assassinated, Peace Corps, New Frontier | b. Gerald Ford |
| **3.018** | _____ | Escalated U.S. involvement in Vietnam, passed Civil Rights laws | c. Lyndon Johnson |
| | | | d. Ronald Reagan |
| **3.019** | _____ | Began *perestroika* and *glasnost* in U.S.S.R. | e. Martin Luther King |
| **3.020** | _____ | U.S. war hero, Desert Storm | f. George H. W. Bush |
| **3.021** | _____ | Strongman drug trafficker, Panama | g. Mikhail Gorbachev |
| **3.022** | _____ | U.S. war hero, World War II and Korea | h. Boris Yeltsin |
| **3.023** | _____ | Appointed vice president, became president by Nixon's resignation, *Mayaguez* | i. Norman Schwarzkopf |
| | | | j. Saddam Hussein |
| **3.024** | _____ | Dictator of Cuba | k. Manuel Noriega |
| **3.025** | _____ | Communist leader of North Vietnam | l. Douglas MacArthur |
| **3.026** | _____ | Human rights was the key to his foreign policy | m. Fidel Castro |
| **3.027** | _____ | Civil Rights leader, "I Have a Dream" | n. Ho Chi Minh |
| **3.028** | _____ | Very anti-communist, tried to reduce the size of the U.S. government | o. John Kennedy |
| **3.029** | _____ | Savings and Loan Crisis, formed coalition for Desert Storm | |
| **3.030** | _____ | President of Russia, led anti-communist reformers when communists tried to retake the U.S.S.R., 1991 | |

**Check the items that were causes of the event** (1 point for each letter).

**3.031** Fall of communism in Europe and the Soviet Union

   a ☐ Gorbachev came to power

   b. ☐ Brezhnev was elected president

   c. ☐ Soviet economy was in trouble in the 1980s

   d. ☐ Berlin Wall was destroyed

   e. ☐ Anti-communist demonstrations

**3.032** Civil Rights Reforms

   a. ☐ *Brown v. Board of Education*

   b. ☐ Work of Booker T. Washington

   c. ☐ Warsaw Pact

   d. ☐ Lyndon Johnson's legislative skill

   e. ☐ Sit-ins

   f. ☐ March on Washington

   g. ☐ Busing

   h. ☐ Gulf of Tonkin Resolution

   i. ☐ non-violent protests

   j. ☐ Election of Jimmy Carter

**3.033** Increased Cold War Tensions

   a. ☐ U-2 Affair

   b. ☐ Bay of Pigs

   c. ☐ NATO

   d. ☐ SALT

   e. ☐ Détente

   f. ☐ Stagflation

   g. ☐ Desert Storm

   h. ☐ Berlin Wall

   i. ☐ Tet Offensive

   j. ☐ Iran-Contra Affair

80/100  SCORE _____  TEACHER _____ _____
initials    date

**Before taking the LIFEPAC Test, you may want to do one or more of these self checks.**

1. _____   Read the objectives. See if you can do them.
2. _____   Restudy the material related to any objectives that you cannot do.
3. _____   Use the **SQ3R** study procedure to review the material.
4. _____   Review activities, Self Tests, and LIFEPAC vocabulary words.
5. _____   Restudy areas of weakness indicated by the last Self Test.